3L8— 4382 men
3L8 — 5753

Teachers
and Machines
The Classroom Use of Technology Since 1920

D0219021

Officially Withdrawn

TEACHERS AND MACHINES

The Classroom Use of Technology Since 1920

LARRY CUBAN

Stanford University

TEACHERS COLLEGE PRESS

Teachers College, Columbia University
New York and London

Published by Teachers College Press, 1234 Amsterdam Avenue,
New York, N.Y. 10027

COPYRIGHT © 1986 BY TEACHERS COLLEGE, COLUMBIA UNIVERSITY

All rights reserved. No part of this publication may be reproduced or transmitted in
any form or by any means, electronic or mechanical, including photocopy, or any
information storage and retrieval system, without permission from the publisher.

LIBRARY OF CONGRESS CATALOGING
IN PUBLICATION DATA

Cuban, Larry.
  Teachers and machines.

  Bibliography: p.
  Includes index.
    1. Educational technology—History. 2. Educational
broadcasting—History. I. Title.
LB1028.3.C8 1985   371.3'07'8   85-14789

ISBN 0-8077-2792-X (pbk.)

MANUFACTURED IN THE UNITED STATES OF AMERICA

91 90 89 88 87   2 3 4 5 6

To all the wonderful women in my life:
Barbara, Sondra, Janice, and Anne Smith

Contents

Epilogue   **104**

Acknowledgments

This book grows out of a wedding between research and experience. I taught for fourteen years in inner-city high schools and used machines no more frequently than most of the teachers in this study. Nonetheless, I remained intrigued by the possibilities for the use of machines, especially for the use of television. When I became a superintendent, my interest in the impact of television on children deepened considerably, to the point of my chairing a citizens' panel that advised a Washington, D.C., commercial station on its programming.

When I came to Stanford University, I pursued that interest by exploring the history of television use in schools with the help of a grant from the Spencer Foundation. When I completed that study, my training as a historian spurred me to ask whether what I had found with teacher use of television was similar to or different from teacher use of film and radio —two earlier machine technologies. Researching those technologies in the midst of the crescendo of noise surrounding desktop computers, I decided to add a final chapter on the most recent machine to enter classrooms.

To Leslie Taylor, who helped me research the study on instructional television, I extend my thanks for her quiet persistence, diligent follow-through, and insightful suggestions. She was a first-rate research assistant. David Tyack and Decker Walker read portions of the final manuscript, and their comments reflected engagement with the material even though they both disagreed with some of my interpretations. Of course, I hold them blameless for any errors in either fact or interpretation. I do appreciate their seriousness and concern.

In many ways, this book continues my reconstruction of what teachers have done in classrooms over the last century. Determining what tools teachers used and why may help practitioners, researchers, and policymakers understand better the classroom as a workplace.

Introduction

Some images stick in the mind like a thistle to a pant leg. A few years ago, while researching how teachers taught in the 1920s, I came across a 1927 National Archives photograph of a Los Angeles teacher in the midst of a geography lesson in the cabin of an airplane (shown on page 8). Here was an aerial classroom of students viewing urban geography firsthand; this was to demonstrate clearly how progressive education had influenced the city's teacher corps. In the photo, the teacher, standing in the front of the cabin near a small chalkboard, pointed to a globe as she talked to seven children sitting two abreast in desks facing her. The juxtaposition of an aerial classroom, the apex of modern technology in 1927, with a teacher, instructing the class in a totally earthbound, familiar manner, seemed to be a symbolic shorthand for the perennial paradox facing public schools: constancy amidst change.

Over the last century, public schools have modified their governance, programs, curricula, organization, and instruction in varying degrees. Moreover, critics often have pointed out how vulnerable schools have been to shifts in educational fashions. Fads, like changing dress hemlines and suit lapels, have entered and exited schools, yet these very same schools have been the targets of persistent criticism over their rigidity and resistance to reform. "It is easier to put a man on the moon," Massachusetts Institute of Technology professor Jerrold Zachiarias said in 1966, "than to reform public schools."[1] Almost two decades later, retired Admiral Hyman Rickover said, "Changing schools is like moving a graveyard."[2] In the press toward improvement that has characterized most studies of public schools, few writers have noted that both constancy and change, entangled together, capture the complexity of schooling far better than the usual either/or dichotomy posed by reformers.

Nowhere is this paradox more apparent than in the interplay between the classroom teacher and technology. Since the mid-nineteenth century the classroom has become home to a succession of technologies (e.g., textbook, chalkboard, radio, film, and television) that have been tailored to the dimensions of classroom practice. Yet the teacher has been singled out as inflexibly resistant to "modern" technology, stubbornly engaging in a closed-door policy toward using new mechanical and automated instructional aids.[3]

In trying to understand the anatomy of this paradox, I begin with the classroom as the crucible where conflicting cultural, community, and organizational imperatives mix, creating the elements of the paradox. In the books they use, the curricula they follow, their pedagogical choices, and the goals they pledge to achieve, teachers cope with contradictory social messages. Embedded in the policies, work routines, and expectations signaled by administrators, school boards, media, and parents is a set of contradictory notions:

- Socialize all children, yet nourish each child's individual creativity.
- Teach the best that the past has to offer, but insure that each child possesses practical skills marketable in the community.
- Demand obedience to authority, but encourage individual children to think and question.
- Cultivate cooperation, but prepare children to compete.[4]

Coping with these conflicting messages within the hierarchical structures in which teachers must work drives them to construct a practical pedagogy, permitting them to complete a hectic five-hour instructional day. Reduced to classroom scale, teacher-invented solutions to these contradictions often have concentrated on transferring knowledge, skills, and values to students through the teacher lecturing and questioning while the student listens and answers, and through reading textbooks and performing chalkboard and other in-class work. This pedagogy worked. It has provided continuity between generations while presumably laying the foundation for individual change in children. Yet shifting public expectations for what schools should achieve (e.g., high test scores) leaves teachers consistently open to attack.[5]

Conveying information highly prized by community decision makers emerged early as a practical solution teachers invented to meet cross-cutting demands placed upon them. What is acquired in classrooms could be verified by community elders and offered by the school as tangible evidence of learning. Passing on knowledge to students is the force that drives the engine of instruction. The question thus becomes *how* to teach information efficiently. Is there any mechanical or electronic device that is less costly than a teacher's voice, with a class of thirty or more?

For years, educators searched for means of communicating knowledge in simple, inexpensive, and timely ways. "The best education," Alfred North Whitehead said, "is to be found in gaining the utmost information from the simplest apparatus."[6] Many educators have dreamed of making instruction both productive and enriching; wishing that children somehow could learn more and faster while teachers taught less. In any list of explanations for the errant passion for technology by educators (but not necessarily teachers), a solid candidate would be this dream of increasing productivity, that is, students acquiring more information with the same or even less teacher effort. This dream has persisted from the invention of the lecture centuries ago to the early decades of this century when reformers sought efficiency through film, radio, and television. The dream persists into the 1980s with promoters boosting desk-top computers for each student. In the insistent quest for increased productivity and efficiency, the lecture, film, radio, television, and microcomputer are first cousins.[7]

Chalk and slate, books and pictures were nineteenth-century media used to expand the sole medium of instruction

—teacher talk—into a broader array of visual tools for conveying facts, skills, and values. More recently, films, radio, tape recorders, television, and computers have entered the teacher's cupboard to be counted as automated and electronic teacher helpers. The promises implied in these aids caught educators' attention: individualized instruction, relief of the tedium of repetitive activities, and presentation of content beyond what was available to a classroom teacher. What I define as useful instructional technology, then, is any device available to teachers for use in instructing students in a more efficient and stimulating manner than the sole use of the teacher's voice. Hardware and software, the tool itself, and the information the tool conveys define the technology (i.e., the book is the hardware, the contents are the software, the radio set is the tool, and the program is software).[8]

There is little that is novel in these assertions or in the narrow definition of instructional technology. The constant search for efficient classroom instruction and the preceding definition of technology merely underscore basic impulses that have entangled professionals in their fickle romance with film, radio, television, and computer-assisted instruction.[9]

Calling the relationship between educators and technology a "fickle romance" attempts to capture the paradox of stability and change in classrooms. What has been written about motion pictures, radio, and television has concentrated primarily upon what the new device could do to revolutionize (a word frequently used by promoters of technology) the classroom. In reviewing the literature on technology in classrooms, I found definite patterns in both academic and popular writings that pursued an unrelenting cycle.

Claims predicting extraordinary changes in teacher practice and student learning, mixed with promotional tactics, dominated the literature in the initial wave of enthusiasm for each new technology. Seldom were these innovations initiated by teachers. As early as the 1920s, one teacher wrote a poem entitled "Antiquated."

Mr. Edison says
That the radio will supplant the teacher.

Already one may learn languages by
    means of Victrola records.
The moving picture will visualize
What the radio fails to get across.
Teachers will be relegated to the backwoods,
With fire-horses,
And long-haired women;
Or, perhaps shown in museums.
Education will become a matter
Of pressing the button.
Perhaps I can get a position at the
    switchboard. [10]

Reformers, more often than not, were foundation executives, educational administrators, and wholesalers who saw solutions to school problems in swift technological advances. Not long after each innovation was introduced came academic studies to demonstrate the effectiveness of the particular teacher aid as compared to conventional instruction. Invariably, the mechanical or electronic device proved as effective as a teacher in conveying information to students. Marring the general favor and scientific credibility enjoyed by the innovation, however, would be scattered complaints from teachers or classroom observers about the logistics of use, technical imperfections, incompatibility with current programs, or similar concerns. At a later point, surveys would document teacher use of the particular tool as disappointingly infrequent. Such surveys would unleash mild to harsh criticism of administrators who left costly machines in closets to gather cobwebs, or stinging rebukes of narrow-minded, stubborn teachers reluctant to use learning tools that studies had shown to be academically effective. Once limited classroom use had been established, teacher-bashing (as the British label it) produced a series of sharp critiques blaming intransigent teachers for blocking improvements through modern technology. Few scholars, policy makers, or practitioners ever questioned the claims of boosters or even asked whether the technology *should* be introduced.

The exhilaration / scientific-credibility / disappointment /

teacher-bashing cycle described here drew its energy from an unswerving, insistent impulse on the part of nonteachers to change classroom practice. Reformers branded stability in teacher practice as inertia or knee-jerk conservatism. They viewed teacher reluctance as an obstacle to overcome. Seldom did investigators try to adopt a teacher's perspective or appreciate the duality of continuity and change that marked both schools and classrooms. Nor did any reformer even raise the disturbing issue that teacher expertise, drawn from a pool of craft wisdom about children and schooling that dances beyond the limited understanding of nonteaching reformers, should be bolstered rather than belittled.

In an effort to understand how teachers responded to three new technological devices touted as panaceas to cure educational ills, I studied the introduction of film and radio in the classroom after 1920. Generally using secondary sources and primary ones where appropriate, I reconstructed the hoopla and actual teacher usage of these media until the introduction of instructional television in the mid-1950s. Then I investigated classroom television, an innovation that now has been used for over three decades in the nation's schools. In examining these technologies, I asked questions that probed why teachers have used radio, film, and television as they have.

Three questions guided this investigation:

1. Once the new technology was adopted by school districts as appropriate for children, to what degree did teachers use film, radio, and instructional television?
2. What explains the degree of teacher use of these technologies since the 1920s?
3. Based upon patterns in teacher use of film, radio, and classroom television, what is the likely level of teacher use of computers in the 1980s, and what is the potential influence of this technology?[11]

In answering these questions, however tentative such answers may be, I offer a view from the classroom rather than from the school board or superintendent's office. I do so consciously in an effort to correct an unhealthy imbalance in most writing about classroom reform, which ignores the teacher's perspective. Furthermore, I wish to underscore the persistent interplay between constancy and change in the nation's classrooms. In this process, perhaps respect can be restored for the notion that stability in teaching practice and the craft of instruction are positive forces in schools, maintaining a delicate balance amidst swiftly changing public expectations.

New York Times *No. 306-NT-520A-6 in National Archives*

"To-day's Aerial Geography Lesson"

1/ Film and Radio

The Promise of Bringing the World into the Classroom

I believe that the motion picture is destined to revolutionize our educational system and that in a few years it will supplant largely, if not entirely, the use of textbooks.

I should say that on the average we get about two percent efficiency out of schoolbooks as they are written today. The education of the future, as I see it, will be conducted through the medium of the motion picture ... where it should be possible to obtain one hundred percent efficiency.

THOMAS EDISON, 1922

TEACHING AT THE TURN OF THE CENTURY

By 1900, public schools had established organizational and classroom practices that would be familiar to present-day observers. Schools usually were divided into grades and separate classrooms, one to a teacher. Rows of desks bolted to the floor faced a chalkboard and teacher's desk (portable desks were installed in the early 1900s but did not become common until the 1930s). Courses of study set the boundaries and expectations for what had to be taught and when. Report cards, homework, textbooks, teacher lectures, and student recitation were standard features of urban classrooms at the turn of the century.

What did teachers do in their classrooms? According to critics, instruction was regimented, mechanical, and mindless. Teachers, according to one researcher, told students "when they should sit, when they should stand, where they

9

should hang their coats, when they should turn their heads."
Students entered and exited classrooms, rose and sat, wrote
and spoke—as one.[1]

Photographs of elementary school classrooms in these
years typically show rows of children with hands folded atop
their desks staring into the camera with a teacher standing
nearby. One photo of a Washington, D.C. class shows twenty-
seven children sitting at their desks, cheeks puffed up, ready
for the teacher's command to blow on pinwheels held in their
hands.[2]

Evidence drawn from various sources documents classrooms taught in a uniform manner. "Passive, routine,
clerical," a school superintendent reported in his visit to fifty
Portland (Oregon) elementary classrooms in 1913, "are the
terms that most fittingly describe the attitude of principals
and grammar grade teachers toward their work."[3] A Teachers
College researcher visited 100 high school academic classes
between 1907 and 1911 to study the use of teacher questions.
Using a stopwatch and transcription of teacher-student
exchanges, she found that teachers asked an average of two to
three questions per minute. "The teacher," she commented,
"who has acquired the habit of conducting recitations at the
rate of 100 to 200 questions and answers per classroom
period of forty-five minutes, has truly assumed the pace that
kills." Teachers, she found, talked 64 percent of the time. Of
the remainder that belonged to student talk, much of it was
one-word or short-sentence responses.[4]

Progressivism challenged the formal, mechanical, and
lifeless instruction described by critics in so many classrooms. Pedagogical progressives called for instruction that
built upon student interests, that opened up classroom
windows to the larger world, and that plunged students into
activities that had intellectual and social outcomes. The
teacher's role was to be coach and adviser, not drill sergeant.
Classroom activities embraced projects that students and
teachers jointly determined and explored; there was to be
much interplay among students and much physical movement in the room.[5]

But there was also another branch to the progressive

movement anxious to alter schooling. Anchored in the enthusiasm for scientific management at the turn of the century, adherents of Frederick Taylor entered schools in quest of efficiency. Professors and efficiency engineers undertook time-and-motion studies. They applied especially constructed score cards filled with quantitative measures for school districts hungry to embrace current innovations targeted at cutting costs while boosting productivity. Was teaching Latin more efficient than home economics? Did memorizing equations produce more student knowledge than homework? Were gang toilets more efficient than a bathroom in each elementary classroom? Such were the questions that educational engineers asked.[6]

These efficiency-minded progressives, along with their pedagogical cousins, left their footprints on school districts across the nation. The work of such child-centered reformers as John Dewey and William H. Kilpatrick and dozens of progressives interested in productivity had launched a movement in the early decades of this century that, according to *Time* magazine in 1938, "had touched every school in the U.S."[7]

FILM USE IN THE CLASSROOM

History

Thomas Edison's enthusiasm for films began earlier than the 1922 quote that begins this chapter. "Books will soon be obsolete in the schools," he said in 1913. "Scholars will soon be instructed through the eye. It is possible to touch every branch of human knowledge with the motion picture."[8]

Because the film was viewed as real and concrete, a medium for breathing reality into the spoken and printed word that stirred emotions and interest while taking up far less instructional time, promoters and school officials joined progressive reformers in introducing motion pictures into classrooms. To do so, films had to be created, catalogued, evaluated, and made available (along with equipment) to school districts. Silent commercial films entered American culture in the late 1890s and early 1900s. Films for class-rooms, both commercial and noncommercial, were produced in the first decade of this century. As early as 1910, George Kleine published a 336-page *Catalogue of Educational Motion Pictures*, listing over 1,000 film titles that could be rented by schools. The Young Men's Christian Association published a catalogue in 1914. An early rental library holding films was owned by Thomas Edison.[9]

Because of cost, limited access to prints of films, un-reliable projectors, and other hardware difficulties, individual teachers seldom secured films. The earliest use of film in the classroom was a novelty with no organizational support behind it. School boards and superintendents decided whether or not to introduce film in a district by allocating equipment funds and assigning administrative personnel to handle the function. Hence, city school districts—organiza-tions with larger pools of available dollars and people—tended to be the first places to decide to use this technological innovation.

According to Paul Saettler, the first school use of motion pictures was in 1910, by the Rochester, New York public schools, whose school board adopted films for regular instructional use. In 1917, the Chicago schools organized a "visual education" department. In the years following World War I, many city school districts established similar bureaus. By 1931, twenty-five states had units in their departments of education devoted to films and related media. Early textbooks in the use of motion pictures furthered the influence of film, as did film-oriented college courses for teachers, which appeared in the 1920s.[10]

Classroom use of films became a symbol of progressive teaching approaches, just as the microcomputer is today. In the 1920s and 1930s, the black window shades, silver screen, and 16mm projector lent an aura of modernity and innova-tiveness to classrooms.

The tangled history of how silent films gave way to sound, of mechanical glitches slowing classroom use of motion pictures, of frequent squabbles over the quality of

Reprinted from Working Together (A Ten Year Report): Districts 23 and 24 *(New York, 1937).*

"Proud to Manage the Machines"

commercial films for classroom use, and of bitter competition among educational film businesses has been told elsewhere. What I will do is concentrate upon the early research findings on classroom use.[11]

Effectiveness and Frequency of Use

Academic research on film use has focused on the effectiveness of the technological innovation when compared to conventional instruction. Research designs in the early decades of this century invariably included the use of an "experimental" group and a "control" group. The experimental group or class was shown a film on a topic covered by both sets of classes, while the control group did not see the film. The outcome measurement was an achievement test. Without entering into the familiar debate concerning the substantial weaknesses of this particular methodology as applied to classroom research (a point I raise again in the research undertaken after instructional television was launched), the results are that numerous studies in the 1920s and 1930s proclaimed consistently that films motivated students to learn. Experimental classes registered test scores that were either superior or equal to results achieved by classes where films were absent from teacher instruction.[12]

Whether or not the methodology was flawed or the correlational findings were converted too quickly into cause-effect relationships is of less importance than observing that in the 1920s and 1930s researchers, policy makers, and informed practitioners *believed* that the research demonstrated the motion picture's superiority as a teaching tool. Did these beliefs influence teacher use?

Finding out how many teachers used films in their classrooms, for what purposes, and how often is most difficult. For example, use is linked to accessibility. How many movie projectors are in the building, where they are stored, what condition they are in, and film availability all shape the degree of teacher use. Even when accessibility can be determined, frequency of film use cannot. Few studies before World War II sought such information. When researchers did pursue such questions, then and since 1945, most often they asked superintendents or principals about the kinds of films teachers used and how often they were used. Seldom did researchers ask teachers. Thus, in reconstructing patterns of use, I have sought multiple sources of direct and indirect evidence that I believe captures at least a rough portrait of teacher use of films over the past half a century.

The earliest survey of teacher use that I could locate was done in 1933 by the National Elementary Principals' Association, an affiliate of the National Education Association (NEA). The survey was mailed to elementary principals. Slightly over 7 percent of the members replied. They reported that teachers used silent films in 52 percent of the 366 elementary schools that responded. Only 3 percent reported using sound films, an innovation barely five years old in the commercial market.[13]

In 1946, the NEA conducted a formal survey of more than 1,000 urban and rural school districts, or about one-fifth of

Reprinted from the Thirty-ninth Annual Report of the
Superintendent of Schools, 1936–1937 (New York,
1937). p. 42.

The Film Lesson

the nation's total student population. They sent the instrument to superintendents, who either responded themselves or gave it to the director of visual education or someone else assigned to the task by the school chief. Forty percent of the districts sent the surveys back; the highest number responding (67 percent) came from districts with populations of 100,000 or more. The results shown in table 1.1 use combined reports from the largest districts because of their highest rate of return. The table shows that estimated use was highest in elementary school and declined sharply as students moved into secondary school.[14]

Eight years later, in 1954, NEA tried again. This time they sent surveys only to urban superintendents and asked them to have the adminstrator in charge of audiovisual programs complete the questionnaire. While 78 percent of the largest districts replied, only 34 percent of all urban districts answered the NEA request. Table 1.2 shows the results from the largest districts only.[15]

TABLE 1.1   Estimated Teacher Use of Films by Level, 1946

	Frequently	*Occasionally*	*Never*
Elementary	37.5%	32.1%	35.5%
Junior High	34.9%	24.3%	39.0%
Senior High	20.7%	29.2%	56.0%

Source: Based on data from the National Education Association, "Audio-Visual Education in City School Systems," *Research Bulletin* 24 (December 1946): pp. 146–148.

Note: According to researchers, these percentages will not add up to 100 because "the reports were compiled in the form of frequency distributions. . . . Subject to the accuracy of the estimates submitted, the medians of these percent distributions indicate the relative frequency of use for motion picture films" (p. 146).

TABLE 1.2   Estimated Teacher Use of Films by Level, 1954

	Frequently	*Occasionally*	*Never*
Elementary	42%	33%	11%
Secondary	23%	33%	19%

Source: Based on data from the National Education Association, "Audio-Visual Education in Urban School Districts, 1953–54," *Research Bulletin* 33 (October 1955): p. 114.

Note: In this second study, there was one category for "two or three times a year," which was less than "occasional" and more than "never." I excluded this percentage. I attribute the sharp decrease in "never" between 1946 and 1954 to the insertion of this category. It also explains why the percentages total less than 100.

Edgar Dale,[16] an advocate of increased teacher use of technological aids, summarizes data he collected from across the country in 1954. He found that Georgia teachers at all levels used about one film per month, per teacher. Thirty-two percent of Georgia teachers reported they never used a film. He also reports a time-and-motion study of 189 secondary school teachers in Michigan, where it was found that "the equivalent of a one-reel film about every four weeks" was used.

Another piece of evidence that I find compelling, given the fragmentary data, is the records kept by the director of audiovisual education in New Haven, Connecticut. In a 1953 study of the effectiveness of films in teaching reading, the records of film orders from 175 teachers in grades three, five, and seven were examined. Just over 1,500 films and filmstrips were ordered in one year by teachers in the three grades. Two-thirds of the orders came from 14 percent of the teachers. The twenty-five heavy users (14 percent) were distributed as follows: eleven in the third grade; twelve in the fifth; and two in the seventh.[17]

An indirect way of determining use is simply to find out how many film projectors were available in schools. The NEA surveys provide little direct information on this measure. The closest they came to such figures was in 1954, when they developed a national projector/student ratio of one projector to 415 students. That figure is not very helpful, however. Those who boosted audiovisual instruction did suggest standards for purchasing equipment, in order to "meet listed frequency of average use." I would expect that such a standard probably would exceed what exists in schools, since it is proposed by believers in the technology. In 1948, one group of professionals recommended one projector for every ten secondary teachers, based on an estimated use by those teachers of one film every ten class periods, or twice a month.[18]

After almost forty years of experience with motion pictures in schools, the evidence, as flawed as it is, suggests that most teachers used films infrequently in classrooms. Films took up a bare fraction of the instructional day. As a new classroom tool, film may have entered the teacher's repertoire, but, for any number of reasons, teachers used it hardly at all. Serious users among those who chose to show films were elementary teachers, while the higher percentages of casual users and nonusers clustered in the secondary schools, especially the high schools. If the fragmentary and indirect evidence is to be believed, one must wonder why teachers used film so infrequently.

Reasons for Infrequent Use

The obstacles to frequent use surfaced in the literature on film usage at about the same time as the claims for its

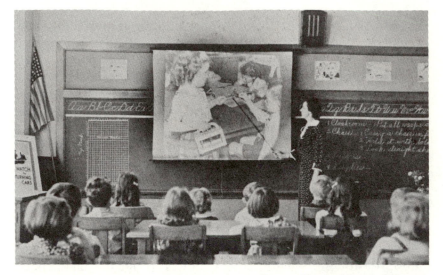

Courtesy Cleveland Board of Education

"Seeing and Hearing the Safety Lesson"

effectiveness. Invariably, the following reasons turned up on lists of obstacles blocking increased film use in classrooms:

- Teachers' lack of skills in using equipment and film
- Cost of films, equipment, and upkeep
- Inaccessibility of equipment when it is needed
- Finding and fitting the right film to the class[19]

Advocates promoted solutions that would eliminate these hardware and software obstacles: courses in teacher education curricula, increasing the supply of films and refining their distribution in schools, increasing the budget allocations for audiovisual education, and similar suggestions.

Thus, on the eve of the introduction of instructional television to public schools in the early 1950s, teacher use of film, while still infrequent after almost four decades of availability, was still the dream of pedagogical and administrative progressives who wanted to make the classroom both an interesting and productive place for learning.

RADIO IN THE CLASSROOM: THE ASSISTANT TEACHER

Benjamin Darrow, founder and first director of the Ohio School of the Air and tireless promoter of radio in classrooms, spoke and wrote frequently about the magic of radio expanding the child's universe. In his 1932 book, *Radio: The Assistant Teacher*, Darrow proclaimed, "The central and dominant aim of education by radio is to bring the world to the classroom, to make universally available the services of the finest teachers, the inspiration of the greatest leaders . . . and unfolding world events which through the radio may come as a vibrant and challenging textbook of the air."[20]

"Textbooks of the air"—that was the dream of scores of enthusiasts, including Darrow, and his successor in later decades, William Levenson, who wrote in 1945, "The time may come when a portable radio receiver will be as common in the classroom as is the blackboard. Radio instruction will be integrated into school life as an accepted educational medium."[21]

Beginning in 1920 when the Radio Division of the U.S. Department of Commerce began licensing commercial and educational stations, classroom broadcasting to enhance instruction spread rapidly in the decades before World War II. The full, tangled story includes problems with federal regulation, commercial development of the airwaves, and uncertainty among educators of which policy routes to pursue. I will concentrate here on the application of radio to classroom instruction and teacher use of this once-novel technology.[22]

Haaren High School in New York City is generally credited as the first public school to use radio to teach a class. Its faculty broadcast lessons to accounting classes in 1923. The Board of Education persuaded WJZ, a commercial station, to allot half an hour each day for educational programs beamed to classrooms and homes across the city. At about the same time in other cities, classroom broadcasting got underway. Dr. Virgil Dickson of the Oakland, California schools began a series of lessons on subjects such as penmanship, arithmetic, and history. Fifty-six lessons lasting twenty minutes each went into classrooms between 1924 and 1925. Chicago station WLS in 1924 began the weekly program "Little Red Schoolhouse." Children and teachers prepared talks on automobiles, farming, science programs, and other topics. Parents supplied schools with receivers. By 1942, in an incomplete survey of school districts across the country, Carroll Atkinson found twenty-nine systems in seventeen states that provided broadcasts at one time or another to classrooms. Of these, Cleveland and Chicago had developed the most elaborate stations, broadcasting schedules, and aids to teachers.[23]

The enthusiasm for radio as a medium of instruction should not obscure the early hardware problems. The principal of Upton High School in Upton, Massachusetts surveyed high schools around the state in 1927 and found that 53 of the 253 schools had radio receivers, of which 29 had been made in the schools. Elsewhere, public schools in Atlanta, Georgia, for example, in 1926 received from a local tradesman one Atwater Kent radio set for each school, "white and colored," in the district. That fall, school opened with morning programs in music for teachers and children. By 1929, however, radio instruction had ceased in the Atlanta schools. The Atwater Kent receivers' batteries needed maintenance during the summer and had gotten none. Students went to the auditorium, but listening proved to be difficult. Almost a decade later, radio programs were reestablished in Atlanta classrooms, this time with battery-less receivers.[24]

By the late 1930s, many of the equipment problems had been resolved, or at least improved. Prices fell sufficiently, so securing sturdy receivers for each school and in some instances for each classroom posed few problems. In 1941, 55 percent of the schools in Ohio had sets.[25] In California, a graduate student surveyed 1,900 schools across the state and found that 66 percent owned one or more sets.[26] Generally, this survey found that rural counties had fewer sets, while city school districts had more.

Local commercial stations and, eventually, national

networks provided classroom programs. In 1928, the National Broadcasting Company began the weekly "Music Appreciation Hour" series with Walter Damrosch, former conductor of the New York Symphony. Lasting until 1942, the program became one of the best known of those produced by commercial networks. The American School of the Air, a program produced by the Columbia Broadcasting System, broadcast its initial program in 1930. Offered twice a week, historical biographies, book discussions, civics lessons, dramas, and current events filled the agenda aimed at both elementary and secondary students. Although controlled by CBS, educational organizations sponsored programs. The Progressive Education Association, for example, supported "Frontiers of Democracy" broadcasts between 1939 and 1940.[27]

State Departments of Education sponsored radio use both directly and indirectly. In the first survey taken in 1932, nine states reported regular broadcasting of short weekly and monthly programs on education. California, Massachusetts, Nebraska, New York, Ohio, and Oregon carried on broadcasting throughout the decade, with only a few interruptions. Except for Ohio, Puerto Rico, Wisconsin, and Wyoming, states that did air instructional programs, most states' activity concentrated on providing information to the public about school curricula, programs, and tests.[28]

Universities entered the arena also. The oldest educational radio station was WHA, owned by the state of Wisconsin and operated by the University of Wisconsin since 1917, when it began broadcasting music programs. By the early 1940s, Wisconsin School of the Air was a fixture in the Midwest. Its eleven series of instructional programs for 1943–1944, shown in table 1.3, suggest the range and audience. The University of Minnesota also produced and aired programs, mostly aimed at high-school students, on its Minnesota School of the Air.[29]

Thus, by 1945, many commercial stations, school districts, state departments of education and universities produced and aired programs for teachers to use in their classrooms. To what degree did teachers use radio? Hardware availability

TABLE 1.3   Wisconsin School of the Air Program Series, 1943–1944

Day and Hour		Series Title	Grades
Monday	9:30 A.M.	Afield with Ranger Mac	5–8
	1:30 P.M.	Exploring the News	5–8
Tuesday	9:30 A.M.	Story Book Land	1–3
	1:30 P.M.	Let's Draw	5–8
Wednesday	9:30 A.M.	Let's Find Out	2–4
	10:45 A.M.	Young Experimenters	5–8
Thursday	9:30 A.M.	Music Enjoyment	1–4
	1:30 P.M.	Men of Freedom	5–8
Friday	9:30 A.M.	Rhythm and Games	K–3
	1:30 P.M.	Book Trails	4–6

Source: Norman Woelfel and Keith Tyler, *Radio and the School* (Yonkers-on-the-Hudson, NY: World Book Co., 1945), pp. 80–81.

suggests far more accessibility to radio programs than film, although no one can suggest that the ultimate in technological saturation that promoters dreamed of—having a receiver in each classroom—was ever reached, except in the rare instance of an occasional affluent district with a school board and superintendent eager for a "radio textbook." Also, the nature of radio programming—half-hour or hour-long broadcasts once a day or a few times a week—destined radio usage to be viewed, at best, as a supplement to teacher instruction.

In determining classroom usage of radio, there are certain problems similar to those encountered with film and others that are unique to radio. As with surveys on film usage, it was common practice for superintendents or their designees to answer the questionnaires. Few surveys ever asked *teachers* what programs they used. The studies that did ask teachers to report use seldom had high rates of return.

Unique to radio, however, was the fact that the size of audience was crucial to commercial success; so many of the surveys were attempts to gauge the number of listeners. In the 1930s and 1940s, this was done by counting either the number of hours aired by the station or the number of students in those schools that had radio sets (thereby assuming that the set was turned on when the program was aired). Hence, estimates of classroom audiences numbered in

Courtesy University of Kentucky Libraries

"With Radio the Underprivileged School Becomes the Privileged One"

the millions. The CBS American School of the Air estimates ran between 8 million and 10 million students listening to its weekly programs. Yet a survey taken of classroom audiences in the year 1940–1941 in Ohio, a state far ahead of others in using radio, found that the American School of the Air was used "regularly" (a term not defined in the survey) by one or more teachers in 3 percent of rural schools, 18 percent of urban schools, 8 percent of elementary schools, and 5 percent of secondary schools. These figures shrank the estimates of classroom audiences to 500,000 to 1 million.[30]

Given these caveats regarding listener estimates, consider the following surveys. In 1937, Carroll Atkinson received a 98 percent return on a survey sent to superintendents in 1,227 districts across the country. He asked: "Do any of your schools use broadcasted features as part of the classroom work?" Just over 7 percent answered that "all" of their schools used radio programs in classes; 17 percent answered "many"; 51 percent marked "few"; and 22 percent said "none."[31] An Ohio survey found that, in the year 1940–1941, 15 percent of the schools "regularly" used radio broadcasts in classrooms.[32] Note that these are responses for *school* use, not for classrooms. If one teacher turned on the receiver in a school of thirty faculty, the school was counted.

In a Wisconsin study of radio use in schools, teachers were invited to have their classes listen to programs. Almost 3,000 teachers asked to be included in the study, received teacher's manuals for the programs, and gave the required tests. Of that number, a sample of elementary teachers was contacted, one-quarter of whom reported their program use to the researchers. Teachers turned on the Wisconsin School of the Air, on the average, three times a week. About three-fourths of the teachers responding to the questionnaire said they used school broadcasts consistently.[33]

Cited as the leader in school broadcasting, Cleveland Board of Education's station, WBOE, offered regular and comprehensive broadcasts covering the entire curriculum in the 1930s and 1940s. William Levenson, in his textbook *Teaching Through Radio*, uses frequent examples of WBOE programming and classroom use, yet in the entire volume he cites only one teacher-use survey, conducted by WBOE staff to determine what elementary-school classes were using the arithmetic program.[34] In that survey the Cleveland school children were grouped into high-, middle-, and low-ability classes. The survey of 115 teachers in ninety-one schools showed that three-quarters of the listeners were in the middle group. Few of the bright or low-ability students (as measured by I.Q. tests) heard the program. Levenson does not tell us whether the 115 teachers were regular users or simply a sample. Elsewhere in his textbook he does claim that, nationally, "nine out of ten American families listen regularly to the radio. Only one out of twenty classrooms do likewise."[35]

Finally, a six-year, foundation-supported study sponsored by the Federal Communications Commission and carried out by the Bureau of Educational Research at Ohio State University evaluating radio broadcasts in the nation's classrooms concluded in 1943 that "radio has not been accepted as a full-fledged member of the educational family." The authors observe that radio spread rapidly in homes but "remains a stepchild of education."[36]

The data are fragmentary. When the studies just cited are connected to data about equipment availability and length of radio broadcasts (half an hour, for the most part), then a faint pattern of limited instructional use emerges. Considered within the context of the six- to seven-hour instructional day, the amount of time spent listening to radio in classrooms before the advent of television is infinitessimal.

Flawed as the evidence is, assuming that it points in the direction of limited classroom use, why did so few teachers use the new technology? A survey of almost 2,000 Ohio principals, conducted in 1941, produced the following list of reasons cited for lack of classroom radio use and the percentage of respondents who gave each reason:[37]

No radio-receiving equipment	50%
School schedule difficulties	23%
Unsatisfactory radio equipment	19%
Lack of information	14%
Poor radio reception	11%
Programs not related to curriculum	11%
Classwork more valuable	10%
Teachers not interested	7%

When the results are broken down, the problems of money and hardware (no or poor equipment, poor reception) pinched elementary schools slightly more than upper-grade teachers, while program content and scheduling blocked secondary-school teachers' use considerably more than their colleagues in the lower grades. These reasons correspond generally to those offered to explain limited film use in classrooms.

Classroom radio promoters, however, were dissatisfied by such reasons for the "widespread neglect of radio in public education" by the end of World War II. The cost of radio receivers, for example, dropped dramatically as they became mass produced in the 1930s and 1940s, so the notion that equipment was too costly for a school district—except for the most impoverished rural ones—is less convincing as a reason for little use. So critics pointed to deeper, more pervasive explanations. Woelfel and Tyler pointed to educators' "indifference and lethargy, even antagonism, toward this revolutionary means of communication." Related to, and perhaps the cause of, this indifference, is the slowness of schools to respond to technological changes in the society. "Radio grew from childhood through adolescence into maturity," they wrote, "too rapidly for organized education, with its fixed courses of study and rules of conduct, to keep pace."[38]

By 1945, radio sets had failed to become "as common in the classroom as is the blackboard." Nor had they achieved this by the 1950s, when the enthusiasm for television kindled the dreams of another generation of school reformers. By then, research and journal articles on radio in the classrooms had virtually disappeared. Few commercial radio networks and stations retained their school broadcasts. The promise of radio as a teaching tool, where "the roof of the classroom has been blown off and the walls have been set on the circumference of the globe," failed to materialize by the time instructional television gripped the imagination of policy makers and educators. Many promoters of radio as a classroom tool, looking forward to television as "radio with its eyes open,"[39] echoed Ben Darrow's prediction: "When the eye and the ear have been remarried in television then we shall indeed be challenged to open wide the school door. There will be no 'blindness gap' to be bridged."[40]

2 / The Use of
Instructional Television
1954–1983

THE BEGINNINGS

Many accounts of the origin of classroom television mark May 25, 1953 as the red-letter day when KUHT in Houston, Texas began broadcasting. Other accounts point to the initial programs that commercial broadcasters beamed into homes early in the morning, such as "Continental Classroom." Or one could go back further and note the closed-circuit broadcasts that the Philadelphia public schools began in 1947 or the Los Angeles high school that experimented with classroom use of television in 1939. These and similar events are just external markers for a number of impulses generated years earlier. These impulses came from veteran radio broadcasters concerned about the number of available television channels being allocated to commercial interests by the Federal Communications Commission (FCC), from impassioned educators who saw much promise offered by the new medium, and from foundation executives concerned about mounting pressures on the public schools from anti-progressive critics of life-adjustment curricula in the 1940s, and from escalating student enrollments.[1]

As so often happens, the impulses that produced the FCC decisions in 1953 to allocate 242 channels for educational purposes were not necessarily the factors that accounted for the subsequent accelerated trajectory in television activity.

Growing criticism of school quality across the nation, harnessed to heightened concerns about overcrowded schools, established a context for identifying improved schooling as a priority, even prior to the Soviets orbiting their satellite.

The Ford Foundation and its Fund for the Advancement of Education underwrote the initial use of the medium in schools and colleges, especially as a tool for relieving the crushing shortage of teachers that resulted from ballooning enrollments. Without Ford Foundation sponsorship, classroom video probably would have remained chic gimmickry not unlike the "talking typewriters" of a few decades earlier. While radio and film received scattered support from public and private agencies, few technological innovations have received such a substantial financial boost from a private organization as classroom television did throughout the 1950s and early 1960s.[2]

By 1961, over $20 million had been invested in 250 school systems and fifty colleges across the country by the Ford Foundation's Fund for the Advancement of Education. Federal aid had entered the arena of instructional technology with the passage of the National Defense Education Act (NDEA) in 1958. In 1962, President Kennedy secured an appropriation from Congress that authorized the U.S. Office of Education to plow $32 million into the development of classroom television. By 1971, over $100 million had been spent by both public and private sources.[3]

Flush times across the country produced consortia for pooling services and regionalizing broadcasts. Interest in joining a movement swept both educators and laymen across the nation. The Midwest Program on Airborne Television Instruction used airplanes to beam signals to classrooms in six states. The National Program in the Use of Television in the Public Schools lobbied school boards and superintendents in ten cities and three states to install and use the medium for large classes and team teaching, as an integral part of the daily instructional program. Articles in newspapers, magazines, and professional journals boosted the merits of classroom television, arguing that its benefits far outweighed any deficits.

By the mid-1950s, a number of school districts using Ford Foundation grants, local funds, and corporate equipment plunged into televised instruction. Basically, district-wide uses of classroom television followed patterns laid down in the first decade of its adoption:

1. *Total instructional program presented by television teacher.* Programs are viewed in small and large classes in which the teacher acts as a supervisor. While there was much written about this as a means of coping with the teacher shortage, the only American school district between 1964 and 1970 that relied totally on television was in the group of South Pacific islands known as American Samoa.[4]

2. *Supplemented television instruction.* The classroom teacher prepares the class for the video lesson and follows up the television teacher's presentation with in-class discussion and assignments. The bulk of instruction remains in the classroom teacher's hands. A small number of school districts across the country allotted up to one-third of the classroom day to televised lessons, especially in the mid to late 1950s, most notably St. Louis, Philadelphia, and the often-cited Hagerstown, Maryland.

3. *Television as a teaching aid.* The classroom teacher controls the content and delivery of the lesson, determining when and under what conditions the televised lesson is brought into the classroom. Usage may be as frequent as once a day or as infrequent as once a month; the pattern of use resembles other mechanical teacher helpers such as films, radio, and tape recorders. This appeared to be the dominant behavior in classrooms since the 1950s although published claims asserted the second pattern of supplementary use to be prevalent.[5]

The first pattern existed only in Samoa and nowhere in mainland America, while the second pattern, although it was infrequently employed, drew the most notice from educators and the media. Therefore, I will summarize briefly a few of the well-publicized efforts within those two areas, to under-score the context, adoption, and implementation of classroom television, before moving on to examine the most widespread teacher behavior with regard to the use of televised instruction.

Samoa

After the distinguished visitor completed his inspec-tion of the new school, he turned to the crowd and said, "Samoan children are learning twice as fast as they once did, and retaining what they learn. . . . [The] one requirement for a good and a universal education is an inexpensive and readily available means of teaching children. Unhappily, the world has only a fraction of the teachers it needs. Samoa has met this problem through educational television." When Pres-ident Lyndon Johnson spoke these words in Samoa enroute to Australia in 1968, television had been in Samoan classrooms for just four years.

Much had occurred in Samoa in the can-do climate of the New Frontier years, following the appointment in 1961 of Governor H. Rex Lee.[6] Education on the islands was in a shambles, conducted in one-room antiquated schools and a few larger buildings, all of which were inadequate to house the islands' 5,100 students. Out of a teaching corps of 284, not one possessed a mainland certificate. Lee made the overhaul of the entire school system his top priority. He rejected the usual strategies of pouring new money into the school system, hiring mainland teachers and retraining Samoan ones, and retooling the curriculum—advice offered by his aides and local educators. He wanted swift and total change. In television he saw the marriage of a new tech-nology with the demand for improved schooling at a reason-able cost.

Within three years of his arrival, Congress approved the Department of Interior's requests for over $1 million in aid. Equipment had been purchased and installed, and elementary students were sitting in front of television sets. By 1966, four of every five students were spending from one-quarter to one-third of their class time watching televised lessons. For elementary schools, the core of the instructional program was telecast lessons. While only two hours of actual watching time was involved, the entire day was built around preparing for the lesson, looking at the set, and following up with related activities. A schedule for September 1965 for grades 7 and 8 suggests the daily rhythm:

7:30–7:40	Opening exercises
7:40–7:50	Study period
7:50–8:00	Preparing for mathematics
8:00–8:20	Mathematics telecast
8:20–8:45	Follow-up mathematics
8:45–8:50	Preparing for sound drill and oral English
8:50–9:10	Sound drill and oral English telecast
9:10–9:15	Preparing for language arts
9:15–9:35	Language arts telecast
9:35–10:15	Preparing for science (M, W, F)
	Preparing for hygiene and sanitation telecast (T, Th)
10:15–10:35	Science or hygiene and sanitation telecast
10:35–11:00	Follow-up for science or hygiene
11:00–11:05	Preparing for physical education
11:05–11:30	Physical education activities (telecast 11:05–11:20, M)
11:30–11:40	Wash hands
11:40–11:45	Preparing for oral English
11:45–12:00	Oral English telecast
12:00–12:30	Lunch
12:30–12:40	Preparing for social studies
12:40–1:00	Social studies telecast (M, W, F)
	Fa'alogo Ma Aoa, a show-and-tell program (Th)
1:00–1:30	Follow-up for social studies; evaluation and dismissal
1:45–3:00	Inservice for teachers, telecast 2:00[7]

Studio teachers, mostly recruited from the mainland, prepared the packets of materials that accompanied all telecasts. These became textbooks. Samoan classroom teachers, seldom involved in the design or planning of the curriculum, were instructed both in print and in televised inservice lessons what to do in preparing for the telecast and what activities to do with children after the program. Classroom teachers became junior partners in a team effort where the studio teacher did all the planning and presenting before the camera and the Samoan teacher dealt directly with the students.[8]

Early reports of the success of Samoan television drew visitors from the United States and other nations. Although pronounced a success by President Johnson in 1968, by the early 1970s strong resistance to continued use of telecasts as the central vehicle of instruction surfaced. In a 1972 survey of student and teacher opinion, both groups expressed substantial reservations about the amount of daily television and its continuation. The pattern was most accepted in grades 1 through 4, but opposition began at grade 5 and got stronger at each higher grade, as both students and teachers criticized existing arrangements. Three out of four high-school teachers and administrators wanted to reduce substantially the level of telecasting. Over half of the elementary students and 70 percent of the high-school students felt that television was used too much in classrooms. Thus, in the eighth year of instructional television in Samoa, most students believed that they watched too much classroom video. Teachers wanted less beamed into the classroom and greater control over the lessons that were broadcast. By 1973, Samoan policy makers had altered the initial blueprint of classroom telecasting, moving to an arrangement that shifted authority from the central studio to the classroom teacher, in deciding whether to use a televised lesson. By 1975, the cutbacks in weekly school telecasts were evident. Whereas in the primary grades in 1965 children had watched almost eight hours a week of televised lessons and high schoolers saw slightly over that amount, a decade later grade schoolers viewed just over five hours a week and central studio telecasts had been eliminated at the high school.[9]

In 1979 when Wilbur Schramm and his colleagues

completed their study of Samoan educational television, the bold experiment offered direct instruction at the elementary level only in oral English, social studies, and language arts for a few periods a week. Upper-grade teachers seldom used television, having shifted instead to occasional use of film or taped broadcasts. "Television's classroom role had been largely reduced," they concluded, "to that of a supplemental or enrichment service, to be used when and if a teacher decided it was appropriate."[10]

Hagerstown, Maryland

In the history of educational fads that have marked the course of public schooling in this country, some small and middle-sized districts have pioneered an innovation and left their names as footnotes attached to certain instructional or curricular improvements. Examples of such names are Dalton, Massachusetts; Winnetka, Illinois; and Pueblo, Colorado. When it comes to television, add Hagerstown, Maryland to the list.

In the mid 1950s, Hagerstown (the city containing the largest number of students in Washington County) proposed to the Fund for the Advancement of Education (FAE) that its school district experiment with closed-circuit television in an effort to meet the pressing needs of overcrowded schools and uncertified, untrained teachers. Over the next five years, the FAE and corporations interested in the experiment underwrote the innovation and spent over $1.5 million. Could the new medium "provide the 18,000 students in the county a richer education, and at less cost, than was possible by conventional methods of instruction?"[11]

Both the FAE and the Washington County schools answered yes. Using closed-circuit broadcasting, teacher planning and inservice programs, large classes for watching telecasts (over 100 students at a time), and more subjects than any previous effort, the Hagerstown experiment ran for five years. By the end of the experiment, over seventy production staff (including twenty-five studio teachers) telecast lessons in eight different subjects (with emphasis on art, music,

science, and arithmetic) at the elementary level and in fifteen
different subjects at the secondary level. [12]

At no point did the promoters of instructional television
see it as delivering the total instructional program. School
officials involved teachers in planning curriculum changes
prior to televising lessons and stressed a team approach
between the studio teacher and classroom teachers. They also
sought frequent teacher assessment of programs and used the
medium for teacher education (e.g., informal learning of new
techniques by classroom teachers watching the studio teacher
give a lesson). Such approaches prevented closed-circuit
programming from assuming too high a profile in the
instructional program. In the year 1961–1962, in elementary
classrooms where the most sets were provided, between 7
and 13 percent of instructional time was spent viewing
telecasts. These lessons lasted from thirteen to twenty-five
minutes and were followed by work under the direction of
the classroom teacher. Junior-high students watched television up to one-third of the instructional day, while senior-
high students seldom spent more than 10 percent of their day
watching lessons; at both levels, viewing often occurred in
large groups of 100 or more students. [13]

Superintendent William Brish and his successors repeatedly emphasized the supplementary role that television
played in the instructional program. Yet the rationale of
saving money by having large classes view telecasts offered
by studio teachers seldom stayed in the shadows whenever
the pros and cons of instructional television were debated.
Instead of hiring itinerant specialists to teach music and art,
master teachers were hired to broadcast certain lessons to
large classes; hence, fewer secondary teachers were hired. [14]

The experiment, from all accounts, worked. Standardized
test scores in arithmetic, science, reading, advanced math,
and other high-school subjects showed dramatic improvements for those students who watched telecasts as compared
to students whose schools, mostly rural, were still unwired;
moreover, Hagerstown students improved their position
compared to national norms. There were methodological
problems, however. The use of standardized test scores

comparing groups where socioeconomic background was uncontrolled went unmentioned in these reports on the effectiveness of classroom television. Avoiding such questions, Washington County administrators collected data on student, teacher, and parent reactions to classroom television. Consensus was clear: all groups favored its use; they found it a worthwhile teaching tool.[15]

By 1963, the verdict was that supplemental use of classroom television through a closed-circuit system enhanced the schooling that students received, saved scarce budget dollars, and improved teacher performance. Nonetheless, FAE funds were withdrawn at the end of the five years, as was private support from the telephone company, which had laid the cables and absorbed the annual cost during the life of the experiment. Funding solely through local resources raised a number of problems with which the Washington County School District wrestled throughout the 1960s.

By 1983, the massive experiment had assumed the familiar, if scaled-down, trappings of a department (Division of Instructional TV) in a middle-sized school system of forty-two schools. The major changes had occurred in the county moving from closed-circuit broadcast and use of telephone lines on a fixed schedule of transmission to taped broadcasts, video cassettes, use of Maryland and national programs, and a schedule controlled by the teacher's flick of the switch on the set. Yet the same supplemental functions of supplying art and music lessons, strengthening professional skills of teachers and administrators, and producing programs in response to teacher demand continued. Strikingly, the annual budget of $334,000 included the reasoning that the Division of Instructional TV was of no real cost to the county because art and music lessons for the primary grades were offered through television, thus saving the county the costs of hiring twelve itinerant teachers to provide those lessons—a common practice in many districts. A 1981 teacher survey in the lower grades recorded beween 90 and 100 percent use of these art and music programs.[16]

In describing instances of classroom television being used as the total instructional program and as a supplement, I emphasize that such cases as Samoa and Hagerstown were in the minority. Few school districts embraced the use of classroom television as ambitiously as these two exemplars. Like its predecessors, film and radio, the dominant pattern for television, even in the 1950s, was as a helper to the teacher. This section will concentrate on level of teacher use, but it is necessary to discuss briefly the role of the teacher as it developed in the 1950s in respect to classroom television.

IMPACT OF INSTRUCTIONAL TELEVISION ON THE CLASSROOM TEACHER

Television was hurled at teachers. The technology and its initial applications to the classroom were conceived, planned, and adopted by nonteachers, just as radio and film had captured the imaginations of an earlier generation of reformers interested in improving instructional productivity. School boards and superintendents initiated efforts for using the new technology; only later were teachers involved in discussions of how to install it into the classroom. Reformers had an itch and they got teachers to scratch it for them. This pattern of bringing teachers in at the tail end of the hoopla surrounding an innovation targeted upon altering classroom practice was common in school organizations. In districts, top-down implementation was the norm for introducing new curricula; new instructional groupings, such as tracking and flexible scheduling; and shifts in the teacher's role, as in open classrooms and team teaching.[17]

The point of all this is to make clear at the onset of this discussion that teachers seldom were consulted or involved in the early stages of introducing instructional television, except as studio teachers or perhaps as writers of scripts or teacher guides. A typical teacher worked in consort with the "master" teacher beamed into the classroom or simply turned on the set and led a follow-up discussion after turning off the program. Teacher as technician would be a fair description of the role envisioned and carried out in the early decades of television's entry into classrooms.

With this point made, let me turn now to how I assess the

impact of instructional television on the classroom teacher since its introduction three decades ago.[18] To do this, a prior and fundamental question needs to be asked: How much did teachers use television? The impact of any technology pivots upon its accessibility, purpose, and use. If a television set sits in the classroom unused week after week, its influence is lost. If television consoles rest on shelves in closets for most of the year, except for infrequent trips into classrooms, the impact of the technology may be insignificant. Thus, teachers are gatekeepers for instructional technology. This is no great insight, yet it is a commonplace observation that is often overlooked. Teachers must open the classroom door for television to enter. Once done, then the issues of accessibility, purpose, and extent of usage emerge.

Accessibility is measured by the number of working sets in the school, the number of teachers who share each set, the level of maintenance of those sets, and the ease with which teachers may arrange televised lessons for their classes. The purposes for using classroom video include delivering the basic curriculum, enriching the existing subjects, and filling up slack time during the day. The extent of usage can be defined by magnitude, frequency, and intensity: how often students watch televised lessons, when viewing occurs, the number and kind of programs viewed, the total amount of time spent in viewing, and whether the program is seen regularly or erratically.

When instructional television first was introduced in the 1950s amidst predicted teacher shortages and demands for improving the curriculum, reformers and administrators saw video as a surrogate teacher. Experiments in Samoa, Hagerstown, and scores of school districts across the nation whetted the appetite of school officials and academics for nourishing the spread of the new technology. While much was said to quiet teacher fears of being replaced by technology, a concerted push by reformers, amplified loudly by the media, sold the new technology as doing many of the things that teachers did and—of even greater importance—what teachers could not do. This initial thrust of the innovation naturally led to a concern for whether or not television as an instructor was as good as the ordinary teacher. Hence, the effectiveness of televised lessons as measured by how well students learn from a televised teacher compared to how well they learn from a classroom teacher became a primary concern in the implementation of the new technology in the 1950s.

Early research on the impact of television upon the classroom, then, was preoccupied with comparisons between televised lessons and conventional teacher approaches, as measured by standardized achievement tests. Generally, the findings concurred: There was no substantial difference between the amount of information learned from televised lessons and information conveyed through conventional instructional approaches used by the classroom teacher—again, as measured by standardized achievement tests.[19]

LEVEL OF TEACHER USE

As the teacher shortage eased in the 1960s and most districts embraced the pattern of television as a supplement to rather than the primary vehicle of instruction, the issue of television as an effective learning tool cooled. Yet, if the impact of instructional television upon children's learning has lessened, the question of video's impact upon teacher practice remains. How much do teachers use television in their classrooms? Researchers know that most teachers use textbooks daily as a medium of instruction; most also use the chalkboard regularly. Yet little information exists that establishes the extent of television use by teachers on either a daily or weekly basis. Frequency of use, of course, avoids the issue of importance; that is, a technology may be used infrequently yet have acute influence upon the teacher and students. Nonetheless, a clearer sense of teacher use establishes a baseline for further exploration of the linkages between teachers and machines.[20]

Surveys of Teachers Use

According to studies based upon self-reports between 1970 and 1981, teachers in three states who said that they used television reported that they watched programs between 2 and 4 percent of the instructional time available to them each week. In other words, teachers turned on the set to watch one or more programs no more than one hour a week. Students spent more time going and coming from the bathroom than watching televised lessons. Recess, collecting lunch money, and pledges to the flag took far more of the instructional day than watching televised lessons.[21] Some teachers never turned to television for lessons. In Maryland, for example, 13 percent of the elementary, 43 percent of the junior-high, and 60 percent of the high-school teachers reported *no* use whatsoever in 1981.

This pattern of greatest use in the lower grades and diminishing use in the higher grades is duplicated in a national study completed by Peter Dirr and Ronald Pedone in the year 1976–1977.[22] The first such in-depth and rigorously conducted study of public school use since the introduction of the medium in the early 1950s, the Dirr and Pedone survey gets cited most on matters touching teacher attitudes, accessibility of the equipment, and patterns of use in schools. Although they used a stratified sample of 3,700 classroom teachers, they asserted with confidence that this sample (and that of superintendents and principals) represented faithfully the nation's schools. In follow-up articles drawn from the study, total populations are reported. For example, 32 percent of the sample of 3,700 teachers across the country were estimated to use instructional television regularly. Dirr and Pedone converted that percentage to the national scale, estimating that 726,000 teachers watched three-quarters or more of all the lessons in at least one series during the school year. Assuming that the 726,000 teachers used television with their entire class, the authors multiplied the national pupil/teacher ratio of slightly over twenty students per class by the number of teachers to arrive at an estimate that 15 million students watch televised lessons regularly.[23]

In determining the frequency of use, Dirr and Pedone reported that teachers averaged between thirty to sixty minutes of television per week in 1977. The highest reports came from elementary teachers (sixty-six minutes a week), with the lowest coming from junior high staff (forty-five minutes a week). Assuming that the typical instructional day is five hours, then televised lessons take up a maximum of 4 percent of the instructional week. Of course, viewing time is only part of a video lesson. Preparation for the program, watching it, and postprogram activities consume a much larger chunk of instructional time, a figure that is not reported in this study.[24]

Another national study concentrated upon the impact of "Thinkabout," a program developed by the Agency for Instructional Television for improving skills of problem-solving and thinking among upper-grade elementary-school students.[25] One set of surveys examined teacher use of instructional video in the year 1979–1980. In a stratified random sample drawn to cover urban, suburban, and rural schools, researchers questioned 731 users and 187 nonusers of "Thinkabout." Most users of "Thinkabout" (66 percent) viewed televised lessons one hour or less a week; for nonusers the figure was 79 percent. The range in viewing, however, extended from ten minutes to 780 minutes a week (yes, at least one teacher reported thirteen hours of weekly viewing). Using the aforementioned assumption about available weekly time for instruction, it was estimated that two-thirds to three-fourths of responding teachers used video 4 percent of the time. Insofar as reported time watching television goes, the "Thinkabout" survey confirmed the results of the earlier Dirr and Pedone study.

The five surveys I have mentioned here, of public school teachers using classroom video covering two states, one city, and the nation between 1970 and 1981, report data that converge across time and setting. Most teachers seldom use the medium. When teachers do use television, they do so infrequently and for only a tiny fraction of the instructional day. The teachers who do use the medium are found most often in the elementary grades and least often in high school. These surveys document a restricted, supplementary use of video that is similar to the use of radio, films, overhead projectors, records, and other audiovisual machines.

Do other investigations of teacher use turn up similar

findings? One source of data I offer now was less the result of a formal study and more the consequence of my extensive classroom visits as superintendent in Arlington, Virginia. The notes I kept resulted from random, unannounced visits to classrooms during which I recorded the activities under way in the room; I used these notes later to write a note to the teacher. Each of the years I served, the Arlington School Board employed, on the average, 1,000 teachers in both elementary and secondary schools. The order of visits and the note taking was unsystematic, since the purpose was far removed from studying teacher use of technology. What the notes do record, however, is the task that the students and teachers were engaged in when I arrived. In reviewing my notes from 549 classrooms of 317 teachers in 25 elementary and secondary schools between 1975 and 1981, I found 11 classes, or 2 percent of the teachers, using television as I entered the room or while I sat there. Eight percent of the teachers used some audiovisual technology (films, slides, overhead projector, tape recorder, and television). Over half of the use of films and television occurred in the afternoon, and it was done far more often at the elementary than secondary level. I offer these data because such direct observation of a large number of classrooms in one district is unusual. The unsystematic collection of the data weakens the overall persuasiveness, however. Alone, these data are curious. In combination with other direct observations of teacher use, such data may move from simply curious information to persuasive evidence.

Observing Two Schools

In order to explore rather than confirm or challenge the accuracy of these findings drawn from surveys and uneven direct observation, my research assistant and I located two schools in the San Jose area that were viewed as exemplary insofar as teacher use of instructional television was concerned. These are presented in the following cases. All names given are pseudonyms.

Fox Elementary School

Fox Elementary is nestled in a quiet, residential area serving middle-income, white-collar, professional, and business families working in what has become nationally known as Silicon Valley. Built in the style of California schools, Fox Elementary has fifteen classrooms, all on one level and all opening directly onto lawns or covered walkways. These classrooms, which house almost 400 children, are divided into wings. There is ample space for outdoor activities. The soothing beige color of the paint covering the exterior walls hides the inexpensive construction materials that went into the building of the school.

Completed in 1961, the six-grade school (including kindergarten) has on its staff a former sixth-grade teacher, Don George, who, after teaching at Fox, went on to become an assistant principal at a nearby junior high school and returned to Fox as principal in 1978. Before entering teaching, George was a radio announcer. His interest in media has continued as a teacher and an administrator, he serves occasionally as a host for programs on the educational channel and has participated in a summer institute on television at a local university. George sees television as "another mode of learning that is valuable because kids are oriented to the electronic age." Yet he recognizes the problem of excess. "It has great possibilities," George says, "but can turn into video valium easily."

Because of his acceptance of video as a tool for learning, George decided to purchase four color sets out of instructional funds when the Santa Clara County Office offered new equipment for sale at cut-rate prices. In addition, he suggested to the Fox Elementary Home-School Club, a group composed of parents, that the school could use another color set. They donated one to the school. He also brought in staff from a public TV station to promote the use of instructional television. Sensitive to the professional autonomy of teachers as to what they should use in their classrooms, George, who himself used television with his sixth grade, treads a narrow line between encouragement and neutrality in his behavior with the thirteen teachers at Fox.

At the time of our study, the week of April 5–9, 1983, seven of the thirteen teachers had signed up for the use of the five color sets, all of which are on mobile carts that can be wheeled easily from room to room. Of the seven teachers, six either had indicated the times that they would use the sets during the week or had told us in interviews the extent to which they would use them. Usage ranged from one to just under four hours a week, with the mean just over two hours. The six teachers, all of whom except a first-year teacher had taught for over fifteen years, for the most part had their classes watch programs in the afternoon (79 percent of the time scheduled for viewing). Hence, in a school where the principal encourages teacher use of televised lessons, where sets are available, and where county staff have held workshops with the teachers, the amount of the instructional week devoted to television ranged from 4 to 15 percent, with the mean at 8 percent. Also, we were told by the teachers that their use of instructional television was governed by the scheduling of series and the rhythm of the school year. For example, many of the series ended in March or April, so afterwards they used television less. Similarly, according to Fox teachers, television might be used less at the beginning of the school when routines are being established; or in the mornings when the bulk of the curriculum on reading, math, and language arts has to be squeezed in.

Spruce Elementary School

Similar in both neighborhood and facilities to Fox, Spruce Elementary School also draws from middle-income families living in Silicon Valley. Slightly smaller than Fox, twelve regular classroom teachers instruct just over 325 students. Veteran principal Larry Kahn has led schools in the district for over a quarter of a century; he has been at Spruce for four years. Kahn views the use of films and television in a generally positive manner, although he did express a note of concern that "you can have too many programs." He defines regular use of television as once to several times a week. His support for use of televised lessons extends to his participation on a countywide committee for instructional television, requests for workshops taught by county staff on using video, and the purchase of one new color set. The school has available three sets for the twelve teachers, one of which had been donated by the school's Parent-Teacher Association. No sign-up system exists since the sets sit in the rooms of three teachers who are regular users. When a nonregular user (i.e., a teacher who does not use at least two or three programs a week) wishes to have a class view a lesson, she either contacts one of the three teachers and a cart with the set is rolled into her room, or she brings her class to the room where the set is, if the regular user wishes to see the same program.

Of the twelve teachers on the staff, surveys conducted by the county since 1978 showed that six to seven members reported themselves as regular users, but without any definition of use included. In discussions with the principal, I was told that five teachers view lessons weekly. On the day that I spent at Spruce, I spent time in the classrooms of three of those five teachers, observing the classes as they watched the programs and spoke with the teachers when they were available.

The three veteran teachers (over two decades of experience each) spent from half an hour to an hour and a half a week using instructional television. That translates to 2 to 6 percent of weekly instructional time allocated to viewing programs. Two of the three generally used video lessons for social studies and science, which meant that most of the viewing occurred in the afternoon. When I asked why most of the video lessons were in the afternoon, all three teachers answered that the morning curriculum of reading and math was a mainstay that could not be tampered with easily and, as one put it, "I want to get the kids in the morning when they're the freshest with the toughest."

How Did Fox and Spruce Teachers Use Televised Lessons?

The patterns of viewing were similar at the two schools, with Spruce teachers using instructional television slightly less than Fox staff did. Of course, "use" does not include time spent before and after program for preparation and follow-up discussion. Nor is use of films included in these calculations, although it became evident in discussions and from noticing 16mm projectors in many rooms that films were used about as much as instructional television.

We watched eight of the twelve teachers who identified themselves as regular users in the two schools conduct lessons from instructional television. Two of the eight made some effort either to prepare the entire class for the particular program or to hold a follow-up discussion on the contents of the quarter-hour lesson. The primary-grade teacher got copies of the songs that were to be sung on "Songbag" and placed them on the childrens' desks. For "Let's Draw" she gave out drawing paper before the program and made sure that the class was silent, since the studio teacher was very soft-spoken.

The other teacher who went beyond turning the set on and off had a sixth-grade class. After the students came in from the playground recess at 1:30, the helpers hurried to close the windows, draw the drapes, and switch off the lights to watch "Parasites." It took about five minutes for the students to settle down while the teacher walked up and down the rows keeping the class's attention upon the screen. After the fifteen-minute program ended, the teacher spent another fifteen minutes asking students specific questions about what they had seen and then moved on to the next subject for the afternoon.

Except for these two teachers, we observed no other preparation or systematic follow-up of the lesson's contents. In the classes of the six other teachers, the color set was wheeled into place—front and center of the class, where the teacher generally stood—the lights were dimmed, and, without introduction, the teacher turned on the program and adjusted the set. One teacher who was concerned about television glare arranged his room differently.

At the end of the program the teacher either would mention what the next one would be or simply would state the point of the completed program. One teacher had the class watch four 15-minute programs about science, math, language arts, and social studies, one after the other without discussion or explanation. Another teacher used "Eureka," "Wordsmith," and "Thinkabout" (physical science, language arts, and social studies) in sequence, without interruption. He felt that this was a fine arrangement since "Eureka" was a fast-paced five-minute science program that he could build on during science lessons; while during "Wordsmith" the children were told to take notes on words, which he would review with them later in the week. "Thinkabout" was a favorite with the class, and their interest ran high throughout the showing. He said that "Thinkabout" was self-explanatory, so no introduction or follow-up discussion was needed.

Students watched the programs with levels of interest ranging from mild to intense. Occasional evidence of boredom surfaced in a number of classes where some students read, whispered, or wrote in notebooks, while the program was shown. Teachers, alert to signs of disinterest, cautioned students to pay attention or quieted a child with a finger to their lip, a glare, or a command for silence. One class, however, was shown four programs in a row, and indifference seasoned with bursts of hostility toward the teacher surfaced repeatedly the afternoon that I spent in the classroom. The first-year teacher had a difficult time maintaining control of the sixth-grade class except when "Self-Incorporated" came on with a program about a junior-high student named Jonathan who is continually reprimanded by adults for not following rules. The program ended by asking viewers to think about when they believed they should follow rules, when they should break rules, and what the consequences would be. The teacher switched off the set and began to answer the narrator's questions. About half of the class appeared to pay attention, while the rest of the sixth graders continued to buzz in their groups scattered around the room. Frustrated by such poor response to her, the teacher turned on the next program, "Bread and Butterflies." Of the eight classes we visited, this was the only one with a management problem that even television couldn't solve for more than a few minutes.

Except for the two classes where there was some teacher

planning around these TV programs, I got the distinct impression that the programs were used to break the pace of the day and to give the teachers a breather while holding the students' interest for a brief period. As one teacher put it, "Sometimes the motor needs to idle before it is put back into gear." Of course, the brevity of our direct observation on one or two days could not pick up the linkages that teachers might well have made during subsequent lessons with programs aired previously. A few teachers said as much to us. In my judgment, acknowledging that such connections could be and were made does not weaken the preceding impressions.

Fortunately, our brief visits to two schools were not the only instances of researchers studying the use of television in classrooms. As part of the national study of "Thinkabout," the Agency for Instructional Television also commissioned three ethnographers to describe how teachers across the country used the program.

A Survey of the Use of "Thinkabout" in Six Classrooms

Billed as "the most ambitious use of instructional television ever made," the sixty fifteen-minute "Thinkabout" programs were designed to help fifth and sixth graders "effectively express themselves, manage their own learning, reason systematically, and think flexibly." Accompanying the sixty programs was a ninety-five page teacher's guide that listed points to make, teaching suggestions, program summaries, and so forth. Planning began in 1973, and the program was introduced in 1979 to the thirty-eight consortia of state and provincial agencies in the United States and Canada that had sponsored the production. Involving hundreds of educators and costing almost $5 million in public and private funds, the series was called "a shining example of meticulous planning, design, and execution." In an effort to assess the impact of the series upon both teachers and students, a million-dollar evaluation bid was won by Western Michigan University, with James Sanders and Subhash Sonnad as principal investigators.[26]

Commissioned by the principal investigators, Marilyn

Cohn, Sylvia Hart-Landsberg, and Harry Wolcott completed three volumes of case studies of six suburban elementary classrooms in the Midwest and West.[27] Because the three researchers spent up to an entire school year in these classrooms, their descriptions provide the rich detail and insight derived from sustained and continuous contact that were lacking in the observations my colleague and I made at Fox and Spruce Elementary Schools. I used these six case studies to answer the questions of how teachers used instructional television.

With just six teachers, classroom use still varied greatly in (1) the number of programs used (e.g., one teacher used all sixty; another only twelve), (2) the amount of preparation given prior to the program (e.g., two teachers had preprogram discussions based upon the teachers' guide; two teachers simply turned the set on when "Thinkabout" was scheduled), (3) the provision of follow-up discussions (e.g., all had some level of discussion, but intensity, time, and relevance to program varied substantially, and (4) linkages made to other classroom tasks (e.g., one teacher connected "Thinkabout" content to other units of study; two teachers made vague connections to the program's content in other activities; two teachers made no effort to make any linkages). In all but one of the classrooms, "Thinkabout" was only one of a myriad of optional "things to do"—reading groups, worksheets, Great Books discussions, *Weekly Reader*, art, class meetings, and so on. Only one teacher fully integrated the televised lessons into the flow of classroom tasks for the entire two to three weeks that he used the program.

Except for this same teacher, "Thinkabout" was shown in the afternoon and provided a welcome break for teachers after the often intense pace pursued in the mornings with reading, math, language arts, and the like. "Thinkabout," as one teacher told Wolcott, "provided fifteen minutes twice a week that I didn't have to plan or teach." Afternoons for these teachers also offered far more choice in the curriculum than mornings. Social studies, science, and art were pursued less rigorously than reading and math, and teachers often looked for filler activities. Finally, energy flagged following lunch.

Another teacher said to Wolcott, "Now comes the part of the day I don't like. The afternoon drags on, and I'm tired."[28]

Summary

Determining what patterns of teacher use of television clearly emerge from this chapter's review of surveys and direct observation of classrooms for brief and sustained periods poses few obstacles. While the six "Thinkabout" case studies present few percentages that can be compared to the other studies, the cases seldom contradict or even mildly challenge the findings drawn from those other studies. In other words, the self-report survey results, our direct observation at Fox and Spruce Elementary schools, the unsystematic notes taken by a superintendent in one school district over a six-year period, and the in-depth case studies of six classrooms from different parts of the country converge to produce at least four conclusions:

1. Instructional television occupies a tiny niche of the school day for the teachers who use it. Television has been and continues to be used as an accessory to rather than the primary vehicle for basic instruction.
2. Only a small band of teachers use the medium willingly, consistently, and with enthusiasm.
3. Teacher use of television, while slight overall, is substantially greater in elementary than in secondary schools.
4. Use appears to be more frequent in the afternoons than in the mornings.

The data do not make clear for which subjects video lessons are used most frequently, nor do they show which programs or what types of programs are the most popular among teachers. What kinds of teachers are users and nonusers of instructional television is another question on which the data shed little light.

Little has changed since television first became available to teachers. In the earlier years, reformers and observers noted the infrequent use of televised lessons by teachers. "If something happened tomorrow to wipe out all instructional television," a fervent advocate of the medium said a decade after its introduction, "America's schools and colleges would hardly know it was gone." The current patterns of teacher use described in this chapter exist almost three decades after the introduction of classroom video and multimillion-dollar investments in consoles, coaxial cables, production studios, staff development, and personnel. Apportioning blame for limited usage, while frequently done, is of little interest to me. Rather, I return to the paradox of change amidst constancy that I raised at the beginning of this investigation. I believe that it is more important to understand *why* teachers have behaved as they have with regard to film, radio, and other highly touted instructional technologies, including the present passion for computers in classrooms, in order to inform the next wave of nonteacher reformers who will try to alter classroom practice.[29] I address these issues in the next chapter.

3 / Explaining
Teacher Use of Machines
in Classrooms

It has been found that teachers reject or at least resist change because of failure to recognize the need for improvement, fear of experimentation, unwillingness to give time, and disillusion or frustration with past experiences. In addition teachers traditionally tend to be conservative and usually will not be impressed by the results of investigations and research or new theories of education.

JAVAD MAFTOON, 1982

How frustrating teacher behavior must have been to promoters of radio, film, and instructional television. School boards bought machines, principals installed them in schools, and teachers occasionally used the technology. Passionate advocates of these innovations often saw teachers as intransigent or, at best, reluctant and fearful. When most of a school's staff would embrace the new technology the effort would excite its boosters, like the story of the man who kissed his wife every morning for twenty-four years and finally got kissed back.[1] Teachers would be lauded; the principal singled out for praise; the school would be featured in newspapers and magazines. But such noteworthy praise and articles only have underscored how rarely teachers have used machines in their classrooms since the 1920s. Why?

Reformers had their answers. Some located the problem in individuals, that is, teachers and principals hostile or indifferent to the march of modern technology. Others pointed to clogged bureaucracies that stifled even the most persistent innovator. Somehow the best ideas lost their vitality in their zig-zag journey between adoption by a school district and implementation in the schools. What emerged in classrooms resembled an anemic version of the original dream. Occasionally, voices would be raised that spoke to the inadequacies of the technology itself, both hardware and software. In researching the use of film, radio, and television in schools, I have located arguments explaining the degree of teacher use. The ones I present here have emerged frequently in the published literature on the three media over the last half century.

In mapping out the dominant arguments explaining limited teacher use of classroom machines, I have the advantage of assessing over six decades' experience with electronic technology aimed at altering teacher practice. From that vantage point, I offer in the last section of this chapter an explanation for the strikingly uniform pattern of occasional teacher use of all kinds of machines in this century.

Offering a menu of explanations is important, I believe, since each argument contains within it a definition of a problem and its solution. Reformers intent upon altering teacher practices, or zealots for the next electronic technology, I suspect, will have in their heads one or more of these explanations as they attempt to sell teachers on the virtues of the next machine that supposedly will revolutionize classroom instruction. Even a rough map of the universe of arguments about teacher use of machines, I believe, helps both academics and practitioners to understand the dimensions and complexity of introducing new technologies into classrooms.

ACCESSIBILITY OF HARDWARE AND SOFTWARE

This argument focuses on the problem of the nature of the innovation. Inadequate or obsolete equipment, limited availability of a viable signal, awkward scheduling of broadcasts, and amateurish programs have persistently blocked teachers from increasing their usage of radio, film, and television. One producer of a noted series of televised lessons said in 1966 that "far too much ITV transmits no more than a fuzzy image of a teacher teaching in a traditional way, using the traditional and impoverished resources of the class-room."[2] While this line of criticism targeted the program mediocrity, the more common fault-finding concentrated on equipment: "It breaks down, and there is often no provision for immediate repairs. Not until technical equipment in education becomes as foolproof, teacherproof, and childproof as common household appliances will teachers use it everywhere."[3]

If breakdowns and obsolescence of equipment are one issue, another is the number of radio and television sets and movie projectors that are available. Mounting a couple of sets in the auditorium or cafeteria or putting hardware on a handful of carts to be pushed down corridors makes radio and video programs accessible to teachers who express unusual interest in certain programs, but it instills little enthusiasm in the breast of a casual user who winces at making complex arrangements to secure a console or film projector at 1:45 when the desired program appears. Squeezing programs taken off the air into the packed daily curriculum requires complicated scheduling maneuvers that none but the determined user would wish to negotiate. Secondary schools, with their fifty-minute periods, prevent all but the most dedicated from using machines.

In a carefully designed study of teacher use of video lessons in West Virginia in the year 1977–1978, teachers were asked why they didn't use instructional television more.[4] Four reasons captured over three-quarters of the teachers' responses to the question:

Broadcast time inconvenient	25%
No equipment or facilities	19.5%
No time	17%
Facilities inconvenient	16%

Another study of Maryland teachers in 1981 categorized into three areas the difficulties that affect ITV use across the grades: (1) program scheduling, (2) advance notice of programs, and (3) sufficient time to plan for the program. For teachers, instructional television failed to meet the classroom demands for a flexible, simple, and accessible tool. Token use resulted.[5]

Program quality varied enough to give teachers pause also. Teachers spent time determining which film, radio, or televised program would fit what they were teaching, would hook children's interest, and would be understandable to students. Once the novelty of the medium faded, many teachers, hard pressed to find time for themselves during the hectic instructional day (much less for assessing films and programs in the library or store room), used machines infrequently.

Program availability, quality of signal, kind of sets used, and scheduling issues may well vary by decade and place, but both the ubiquity and frequency of the responses compellingly point to technological deficiencies and the inflexibility of film, radio, and television as explanations for infrequent teacher use.

IMPLEMENTATION OF THE INNOVATION

In this argument, the focus is on flawed implementation. Repeatedly, observers have pointed out that many technological advances adopted by school boards and pushed by university researchers and foundation-funded reformers seldom have remained in classroom use after the novelty evaporated. Radio, film, language laboratories, programmed learning machines, computer-assisted instruction, use of typewriters in the elementary grades—all have been boosted as revolutionizing instruction yet today seldom appear in most classrooms. Such innovations for solving productivity problems defined by nonteachers invariably were mandated into use by district policy makers, not teachers.

The most common direction for school change is, and has

been, top-down. The clear advantage to top-down mandates is the apparent efficiency in introducing technology by fiat. A decision to adopt instructional television, for example, side-steps the often messy, uncertain, and prolonged discussions with principals and teachers over the advantages and disadvantages of the medium's use in classrooms, its application to student learning, and a host of other concerns that invariably surface when the decision-making process is broadened to include implementors as well as central office decision makers. Note, for example, that while Hagerstown, Maryland teachers were involved in producing televised lessons and writing guides for their colleagues, the teaching corps was uninvolved in the deliberations that produced the experiment. Similarly, Samoan teachers were ignored in the early stages of that grand experiment. The pattern of having policy makers determine whether or not radio, films, and instructional television would be adopted was followed nationwide throughout the first decade of the appearance of these technologies. Adoption, of course, seldom predicts the degree of classroom use.

Responses by teachers to these directives aimed at altering their teaching behavior may be explained by the manner in which the innovation was adopted and implemented. Compliance with authority is expected in organizations. To those mandates that awkwardly fit the contours of a work setting or are inconsistent with the beliefs of the implementors, token compliance is a common response. Embracing the barest minimum that is necessary to convince supervisors that the mandate has been executed is common in those organizations where orders trickle down to the lower levels of the organization. Principals, those primary gatekeepers of schoolwide changes, either may distrust the particular technological innovation or may wish to protect an already smooth operation. Token compliance might well be making one or more film projectors, radio receivers, or television consoles available to a staff or just circulating central office information on programs to the faculty. If no projectors or television sets are available within a school and the principal cannot blame the central office, then the school may be vulnerable to a charge of resisting the school board's or superintendent's directive. Minimal compliance produces well-stocked closets, or a gaggle of machines in the rooms of those few teachers who are willing users. Such a tactic of limited availability offers interested teachers the option of using the electronic technology and simultaneously protects those teachers who choose to ignore the machines.

While this explanation concentrates on school practitioners' token compliance with an instructional policy made at headquarters, it also illuminates two beliefs embedded in the thinking of policy makers and nonteaching reformers who steadfastly push technological innovations. First, they assume that the organization is like a military unit in which orders are given from the top and executed with dispatch and fidelity in settings where the service (i.e., teaching) is delivered in a highly decentralized form (i.e., many different schools and classrooms). Second, adopting technological innovations to improve classroom efficiency offers a view of teaching as a mechanical process of applying knowledge, skills, and tools to students. The teacher, in this view, is a technician who can apply new devices to the classroom swiftly and without complication.

Proponents of the flawed-implementation argument, then, point to *how* the technology was adopted and executed as determining the frequency of machine use in the classroom. Views of teaching and organizational compliance ill-fitted to schools and classrooms and married to feckless strategies aimed at coercing teachers to use the innovation explain limited use of the new technologies.[6]

THE CLASSROOM AND SCHOOL AS WORK SETTINGS

In this argument, I focus on how settings shape behavior. "Settings," as Roger Barker noted, "have plans for their inhabitants." How school space is physically arranged, how content and students are organized into grade levels, how time is allocated for tasks, and what rules govern student and adult behavior stem from the original mandate for public schooling: to get a batch of students compelled to attend school to absorb certain knowledge and values while maintaining orderliness. Thus, schools with self-contained classrooms, age-graded levels, standard class sizes, and uniform teaching loads are crafted instruments designed to cope with the mandate.[7]

The classroom, located within the larger school organization, is a crowded setting in which the teacher has to manage twenty-five or more students of approximately the same age who involuntarily spend—depending upon their grade level —anywhere from one to five hours daily in a room. Amidst continual communication with individual students and groups (up to 1,000 interactions a day in an elementary classroom, according to Philip Jackson[8]), the teacher is expected to maintain control, teach a prescribed content, capture student interest in that content, match levels of instruction to differences among students, and show tangible evidence that students have performed satisfactorily.

Within these overlapping school and classroom settings, the argument runs, teachers have rationed their time and energy to cope with conflicting and multiple demands and have constructed certain teaching practices that have emerged as resilient, simple, and efficient solutions in dealing with a large number of students in a small space for extended periods of time.

So, for example, rows of movable desks and seating charts permit the teacher easy surveillance of the room. The teacher's desk, usually located in a visually prominent part of the room near a chalkboard, underscores quietly who determines the direction for what the class will do each day. Class routines for students, such as raising their hands to answer questions, speaking only when recognized by the teacher, and speaking when no one else is talking establish an orderly framework for group instruction. Teaching the entire class at one time is simply an efficient and convenient use of the teacher's time—a valuable and scarce resource—in covering required content and maintaining control. Lecturing, recitation, seatwork, and homework drawn from texts are direct, uncomplicated ways of transmitting knowledge and directions to groups. Given the constraints placed upon the teacher by the daily schedule and the requirements that a course of study be completed by June, these instructional practices permit the teacher to determine, in a timely and efficient manner, whether or not students have learned the material.

This explanation for persistent regularities in instruction stresses how teachers have coped in a practical manner with the complicated demands generated by school and classroom settings, domains over which they have had little control. By constructing solutions in the shape of practical classroom routines and teaching methods, teachers have survived the acute, cross-cutting daily pressures of the classroom; that is, teachers have constructed a vocabulary to match the grammar of the classroom.

Now, how does the use of radio, film, and instructional television fit with this argument? The tools that teachers have added to their repertoire over time (e.g., chalkboard and textbooks) have been simple, durable, flexible, and responsive to teacher-defined problems in meeting the demands of daily instruction. In his essay, *The Teacher and the Machine*, Philip Jackson nicely captures the importance of versatile and adaptable tools.[9] Jackson describes the chalkboard and textbook as instances of these qualties that appeal to teachers. For the chalkboard, the teacher can write, draw, erase, and keep material for days; diagrams, quizzes, assignments, and insights that spontaneously erupt in discussions—all can be scrawled on the board. "Given this flexibility," Jackson says, "it is no wonder that the chalk-smudged sleeve has become the trademark of the teacher."[10]

Textbooks are also versatile. Portable, compact, and durable, they can be read for a few minutes or hours; read once or many times; skimmed or read carefully. All students can be assigned the same sections or different pages matched to varied abilities of students. Read in class, a bedroom, or out on the lawn at lunchtime, the book travels easily. A flexible teaching tool, the textbook easily outstrips a movie projector or televised lesson for versatility in coping with the unpredictability of classroom life.

I already have discussed the limited availability of radio and television sets, the scheduling hassles for programs taken off the air, and the problems associated with clear signals and obsolete equipment. The rich content of films and radio lessons available to the teacher and the exposure of students to televised experiences immediately are diminished, this argument runs, by the inflexibility of technology to fit the hectic rigors of classrooms. Teacher use, then, would tend to be selective and minimal since the innovation responds less to their concerns than other available instructional tools. Thus, the simplicity, versatility, and efficiency of those aids such as the textbook and chalkboard in coping with problems arising from the complicated realities of classroom instruction far exceed the limited benefits extracted from using machines.

THE NATURE OF THE TEACHING PROFESSION

This argument centers on the culture of the teaching profession itself. Teacher selection, training, and experience and the beliefs teachers hold combine to produce a deep-seated conservatism, a reluctance to alter prevailing practices and use mechanical devices in classrooms.

Student teachers, prior to entering the profession, attend schools for over 13,000 hours, largely for the purpose of being introduced to the culture of teaching. Teaching is one of the few occupations where practically everyone learns firsthand about the job while sitting a few yards away, as students, year after year. We all have absorbed lessons on how to teach as we have watched our teachers.

Those that enter teaching are usually young people who are already favorably disposed to schools, acknowledge the limited financial rewards, seek contact with children, appreciate the flexible work schedule, and embrace the service mission built into teaching. Recruitment and selection, then, bring into the profession people who tend to reaffirm, rather than challenge, the role of schools, thereby tipping the balance toward stability rather than change.

Even in college, beyond an occasional course in audio-visual aids that includes the conventional array of films, overhead projectors, televisions, and microcomputers, teacher-education curricula have little to do with the use of media. The student-teaching experience places newcomers in classrooms where, for the most part, veteran teachers only occasionally use films, televised lessons, and overhead projectors. After serving the apprenticeship, it is the luck of the draw whether or not a teacher ends up in a school where media use is encouraged. Hence, there is little in the formal training and early years of a teacher's career that nurtures the use of the newer forms of technology.

Teaching itself nourishes a cautionary attitude toward change and an arms-length response to automated devices. From the very first day of being a solo practitioner, the teacher faces the complicated process of establishing routines that will permit a group of students to behave in an orderly way while the subject matter is taught. The teacher is driven to use those practices that he or she remembered were used in classrooms or take the counsel of veterans who advised their use. Experienced colleagues may help informally and, in doing so, continually expose newcomers to the norms and expectations of the school and what it takes to survive. The folklore, occupational wisdom, norms, and daily teaching practices reinforce what *is*, rather than nourish technological innovation.

Beliefs shaped by these teaching experiences strengthen the satisfactions derived from personal bonds with students and are part of a teacher's unique perspective. Few teachers, Philip Jackson argues, embrace the engineer's passion for speed, efficiency, and accuracy in meeting specific objectives, completing tasks, and producing tangible outcomes. This is not to say that these values are ignored; rather, teachers find rewards in a different set of considerations. "They worry," Jackson says, "more about whether a student is learning how to read than whether he is still confusing 'saw' and 'was.' They are more concerned with seeing satisfactory progress in arithmetic than with mastery of any specific fact." The holistic view, the interest in "broad constellations of competencies, the components of which may be developing at different rates for different students" is what marks a teacher's perspective, he says.[11] Furthermore, because teachers believe that interpersonal relations are essential in student learning, the use of technologies that either displace, interrupt, or minimize that relationship between teacher and child is viewed in a negative light. The holistic view and the belief in the sacred importance of rapport with students as a foundation for learning are harnessed to an assumption that teaching is an art. Improvisation, imagination, tempo, pacing, and creativity outline in a general way the subtle, imprecise, and intangible aspects that pervade teaching.

Also consider the beliefs that many, but not all, teachers hold about television, radio, and films as entertainment media and therefore somewhat tainted as teaching tools. Excessive use of televised lessons or films, for example, casts suspicion on the teacher as being less than professional or simply scratching for filler material. Such beliefs leave little room for gracious and warm reception of technological guests into the classroom.[12]

Because reformers acknowledge that most teachers view the classroom in nontechnical terms, a large body of criticism of teachers as Luddites and reactionaries resistant to progress has arisen over time. Typical of the criticism (although the language is slightly more purple than usual) is Charles Hoban's observation that "the current and historical role of the classroom teacher is highly ritualized." Any effort to alter that ritual is "likely to be resisted as an invasion of the sanctuary by the barbarians."[13] Hoban, who tried to gain teacher support for classroom radio and, later, instructional television, noted that some rituals are unchanging: teacher's control of instruction, tests, grades, rewards and punishments, and face-to-face interaction. Because these are so important to teachers and because any technological innovation will reshape these core processes, Hoban concluded, "Any sudden or substantial reduction of dominance status, . . . any major change in the interpersonal teacher-student communication situation, or any systematic attempt to scientize and rationalize the intuitively determined interaction patterns of the teacher is likely to elicit at least some teacher hostility and resistance."[14]

Because most people usually account for behavior by

attributing it to individual motives rather than the settings within which people find themselves, not unexpectedly classroom teachers emerge as the villains in the saga of educational technology. Teachers exercise free will; they can do what they want. They are free to use the film projector or turn on the console, but they choose not to and so can be blamed for not embracing machines. The argument, then, targets the pool of candidates from which teachers are drawn, teacher training, school experience, and beliefs that teachers hold, to explain their reluctance to use electronic media. To fervent reformers, the culture of teaching gets transformed into such labels as inertia, resistance, or simple hostility to instructional improvement.[15]

ANALYZING TEACHER USE OF MACHINES

I find all of these arguments plausible. Some strike me as more convincing than others, yet none of them are either implausible or flimsily constructed. They are anchored in historical evidence. I believe that individually or taken together they explain reasonably well why teachers have carved out only a tiny niche for electronic technology. Were I interested only in explaining the low level of classroom use, this would be where I would conclude this book. I have other questions, however, about teacher use of television, radio, and film: Why are some teachers, in Harry Wolcott's phrases, "media-philes" and "willing users," while most are not? Why do more elementary than secondary teachers use machines?

In trying to answer these questions, I believe that a clearer picture may emerge of what teachers face daily, and the larger issue of the future role of classroom technology will be clarified further. Doing this also offers the opportunity to construct a necessary synthesis of all the explanations given so far in this chapter, which I will do by building on a study I completed in 1984 on the history of classroom teaching since the turn of the century.[16]

Constancy and Change in Teacher Practice

In that study, one thing I found was that continuity, far more than change, characterized teacher practices. Change did occur, especially in elementary classrooms, where it exceeded by a large margin what happened in high-school classrooms. In elementary classrooms, teachers shifted from total reliance on whole-group instruction at the turn of the century to the use of small groups for short periods of time by World War II. Also by the same time, teachers permitted far more movement of students around the room and a less formal climate pervaded elementary classrooms as time passed. A wider range of teaching activities expanded teachers' repertoires. Elementary teachers arranged classroom space to appear more homelike. While such alterations did emerge, the central core of instruction remained constant, that is, teachers determined what was taught, the manner of instruction, and the materials that were to be used.

In the high schools, however, whole-group instruction remained the norm; rows of movable desks replaced rows of bolted-down desks; little student movement around the room prevailed over the decades; textbook assignments, review of homework in class, and teacher-led recitation continued with little variation, decade after decade. The overall classroom patterns of teaching practice persisted largely unchanged in the upper grades.

In explaining the presence of far more constancy than change in teaching, I have constructed a tentative explanation that I call "situationally constrained choice." It incorporates two of the explanations I discussed in the last section: (1) school and classroom structures and (2) the culture of teaching, including the social and individual beliefs of teachers. I have chosen to weave together these explanations partly because the result matches the evidence regarding the discrepancies in technology use that I found between elementary and secondary classroom teachers, and the differences in which changes those teachers chose to embrace. There is an intuitive factor here also: This explanation rang true to my twenty-five years of experience as a public-school practitioner.

School and classroom structures, I argue, have established the boundaries within which individual teacher beliefs and an occupational ethos have worked their influence in shaping daily pedagogy. Intertwined as these two influences are, I found it impossible to disentangle each and assign it a relative weight of influence. The constraints, pressures, and channeling that the school and classroom contexts generate are the invisible, encompassing environment that few recognize as shaping what teachers do daily in classrooms. It is—forgive the commonplace observation—the water that surrounds the fish. It is difficult to acknowledge, much less analyze, the commonplace—that which is seen daily and taken for granted as an organic, brick-hard feature of the environment.

Consider, for example, the structural differences between elementary and secondary schools. Informed observers often forget the substantial structural differences in time allocation, student-teacher contact, and expectations for achievement that distinguish the elementary school from the high school. Teachers in the lower grades spend six hours a day with a single group of thirty students, while upper-grade teachers have fifty minutes a day with each of several groups. One teacher, maybe two, meet with elementary children for the entire instructional day. Coherence in instruction and clarity in goals is far more possible with children. At the secondary level, any student will face five to seven teachers, all differing in style and expectations and presenting various subject matter. External demands for performance press secondary-school students far more than elementary ones (e.g., Carnegie units, Scholastic Aptitude Tests, College Boards, having skills to get into college or the workplace, etc.). Such structural differences in school organizations help shape teaching practices. Thus, I believe elementary teachers have somewhat more flexibility in varying their pedagogy and allotting time to different tasks than their secondary-school colleagues. Hence, the potential for instructional change is marginally higher within elementary schools.

Within this school and classroom organizational framework, the culture of teaching, itself shaped in part by structural arrangements, further funnels both newcomers and veterans into teaching regularities, where certain "wisdom" is crafted and reinforced as essential to classroom survival. Teachers who copy mentors and former teachers are not displaying merely a knee-jerk, unthinking reaction; their behavior reflects a practical appraisal of what teaching approaches are necessary to survive the year.

What leavens the deterministic drift of this argument is the potential for change associated with teachers' beliefs. Certainly, the larger social milieu shapes belief systems. Moreover, organizational imperatives influence what people think. Yet different ideas about children's development, how they learn, and purposes for schooling beyond cultivating minds permeate the larger culture and penetrate educators' thinking. New and different ideas enter the intellectual marketplace and teachers, like others, embrace, play with, and reject them as they apply to schools.

To appreciate the power of constancy in teacher practice, consider those changes that teachers have adopted and transformed: the confirmation of stability may simply lie in considering what practices teachers have altered. Remember, for example, that whole-group instruction was a nineteenth-century innovation, an efficient way of coping with student diversity. The introduction of worksheets for students to complete in class while the teacher worked with one or more students was a practical solution to a classroom management problem that all teachers faced. The chalkboard and textbook were efficient, flexible technologies providing students with the same information. Some of what were once innovations for earlier generations of teachers became conventional and durable practices for later ones.

Some teaching practices have changed. The changes teachers have embraced, however, have solved problems that teachers identified as important, not necessarily ones defined by nonteachers. Moreover, what teachers adopted buttressed their authority, rather than undermining it. Thus, those technologies incorporated into routine teacher practice responded to daily classroom needs without undercutting the teacher's control of the class. The arguments, then, that hardware and software inadequacies and imperfect implementation drafted by nonteachers can explain the reluctance of teachers to become heavy machine users would have little application beyond the instance of radio, film, and television. Teachers *have* altered their practice when a technological innovation helped them do a better job of what they already decided had to be done and matched their view of daily classroom realities.

Now, what application does situationally constrained choice have to the puzzling questions surfacing in this study of teacher use of machine technology? How does this explanation illuminate such questions as: Why did most teachers hardly use film, radio, and instructional television? Why were some teachers "willing users"? Why do those teachers who used electronic machines turn up more often than not in elementary schools?

I believe that teacher use of machine technology can test how applicable situationally constrained choice is as an explanation for teaching practice. The explanation I have constructed argues that, because of the severe constraints imposed upon teachers by the classroom and school as workplaces and the imperatives of their occupational culture, teachers will seek out those tools that meet *their* tests of efficiency: Is it simple? Versatile? Reliable? Durable? What is the personal cost in energy versus return in worth for students? Will these new machines help solve problems *teachers* (and not nonteachers) define?

For a teacher, the question of whether she can keep the entire class interested for fifteen minutes in the topic of federal policy toward railroads in the twentieth century is a far more pressing issue to resolve than the problem identified by reformers of whether instructional television will reduce the shortage in qualified teachers. Moreover, teachers will use new instructional tools to the degree that the classroom and the occupational culture finds acceptable. Thus, watching an occasional film or televised lesson is within the norm, but two to three movies a day or television three hours daily would seldom be sanctioned by either administrators or colleagues. Researchers call these implicit but powerful criteria that teachers apply to innovations the "practicality ethic." These teacher-constructed criteria seldom enter the twilight zone that reformers occupy when designing classroom changes.[17]

Thus, what boosters of electronic technology frequently label as teacher stubbornness in embracing innovations can be viewed from the perspective of power: Whose questions count? Teachers ask very different questions of new classroom technologies than do administrators, school board members, state and federal policy makers, and scholars. Teacher questions are anchored in the classroom, an arena largely foreign to nonteachers. Because teachers seldom make instructional policy, questions of craft concerning machines in classrooms seldom surface. Policy makers who adopt innovative technologies and ship them into classrooms ask very different questions about productivity, equity, and cost. For hospital administrators to order surgeons to use a new machine or municipal officials to direct city plumbers to use a new tool would, I believe, be viewed as inappropriate. Yet that is what has occurred in the nation's classrooms, and teachers whose questions have been unsolicited, much less unanswered, close their doors and use what fits their students.

Radio, film, and instructional television met only marginally most problems that teachers defined as important. Instructional television, for example, seldom met the test of efficiency that teachers applied to instructional tools. The problems located in software and hardware and scheduling made video an inflexible and less reliable tool, even though it enriched the curriculum. With increasing pressure to cover more content and concentrate on reading, math, and writing, there simply is less time available for inserting films or televised lessons, particularly if scheduling is uncertain. In short, the 16mm film, radio, and video responded minimally to the complexities of classroom instruction. Furthermore, there are many, perhaps a majority, of teachers who believe that classroom motion pictures and video are too much like their commercial cousins. The impulse toward entertainment, they feel, taints any school use of the media. Strong informal norms in schools operate against extensive use of films and television in school.

Why Some Teachers Are Willing Users

Still, there are some teachers who do use media regularly for a part of the school day. There are teachers, for example, who believe that films and television enhance textbook reading and mimeographed worksheets. There are teachers who are deeply concerned over visual illiteracy of so many children who watch hours of commercial television and yet uncritically accept what they see. Instilling critical viewing skills captures the interest of some teachers who squeeze such lessons into their daily schedules. There are some teachers who believe that teaching students to produce television programs and make films are ideal ways of training students to understand the anatomy of the media business and its effects on Americans. For such teachers, television and film help to solve their daily problem of motivating students to learn and of supplying relevant and meaningful content that will get students to reason and solve problems. In effect, the practical criteria these teachers use in deciding what is best for them and students are broader than ones used by their colleagues. Such teachers, however, are in a distinct minority.[18]

Another group of heavy users may have different reasons. Classroom films and televised lessons solve certain classroom problems teachers face. The organizational requirement of an instructional day of six hours, even interrupted as it is by recesses at the elementary level and planning periods at the secondary level, nonetheless is a long, intense period of contact with students. Hundreds of classroom decisions and exchanges with students over the day produce an ebb and flow of energy among both adults and young people. Peak energy periods for teachers and students are in the mornings. The rhythm of the day noticeably slows down after lunch. It is no accident that most elementary schools concentrate their reading, math, and language arts in the morning, with physical education, science, social studies, art, and music wedged into afternoons—if offered at all. Nor is it an accident that teachers resist late-morning starting times for children. The craft folklore on when students are freshest and will learn is clear: mornings, and the earlier the better.

Thus the afternoons generally become times for catching one's breath, treading water, or shifting pace. As one Spruce Elementary teacher said, "Sometimes the motor needs to idle before it is put back into gear." Like other workers, teachers recognize the rhythm to the instructional day. Ask secondary teachers about the differences in their classes after lunch as compared with those in the morning, apart from subject matter or ability level. Ask elementary teachers what kind of activities they plan for the last hour and a half of the school day. Teacher culture and workplace experience, again, need to be heeded. Teachers see afternoons as times for teaching and also as times for taking a break without harming the instructional pace of the day. Thus, after-lunch hours often get filled with less demanding activities. If teachers can vary the pace, renew their energies, and introduce new and different materials, then they and their students can get through the rubber-band intensity of six hour instructional days.

For those teachers sensitive to the rhythm of their school day and in need of a respite, a televised lesson or short film (and for an earlier generation, a radio program) becomes a practical solution to the stubborn problem of energy loss. They need a breather for a short time, in order to launch another lesson; or they need filler material that will plug gaps in texts; or they simply need interesting programs that will entertain for a few minutes. Radio, video, and film, I suspect, function as coping devices that are practical ways of dealing with the structural arrangements imposed upon teachers. In short, while media in classrooms may be inflexible and unreliable, they do offer that teacher cadre of willing users a tiny but important way of coping with energy loss during the day, providing a breath-catching break without calling it so.[19]

Differential Usage: Elementary Versus Secondary Levels

I have already suggested the outline of an explanation for the larger number of elementary teachers using media than secondary teachers. The organizational structure oͥ the elementary school permits far more student contact and alternate uses of time than in secondary schools. In elementary schools, a program on books that cannot be viewed in the morning can be shown in the afternoon when it is repeated. No such flexibility is available in the secondary level, with its fifty-minute periods. Video tape recorders (VTR) can be used to copy programs, but the teacher must arrange for both the taping and the delivery of the VTR at the time when the class is scheduled. Moreover, media lessons in upper grades have to be right on the target for what teachers are studying. There is far less of a pinch in the lower grades to ensure that subject matter be covered in thirty-six weeks than there is, for example, in an eleventh-grade U.S. history course, where the content is likely to reappear on a departmental or districtwide test.

Furthermore, the training and socialization of elementary teachers simply differs in both substance and style from that of their secondary colleagues. You may show third graders a lovely fifteen-minute film on how birds care for their young simply because it is an aesthetically pleasing lesson and because it bears a passing relationship to the science that is done every other afternoon. Not so for the U.S. history class. Few teachers would show "The St. Louis Cardinals in Spring Training" the day after the class dealt with William Lloyd Garrison and the abolitionists.

Summary

Situationally constrained choice offers a perspective on how teachers do, indeed, change over time while maintaining a durable stability in practice. The basis for this perspective is that teachers will alter classroom behavior selectively to the degree that certain technologies help them solve problems they define as important and avoid eroding their classroom authority. They will either resist or be indifferent to changes that they see as irrelevant to their practice, that increase their burdens without adding benefits to their students' learning, or that weaken their control of the classroom. The password that will unlock the classroom door remains in the teacher's head; understanding what questions teachers ask and what criteria they apply is essential to unlocking that door. The power of the classroom and school settings in establishing the boundaries and shaping the practices harnessed to the culture of teaching explain, I believe, a great deal of teacher behavior and varied responses to classroom innovations in general, and technological ones especially.[20]

4 / The Promise of the Computer

> *There won't be schools in the future. . . . I think the computer will blow up the school. That is, the school defined as something where there are classes, teachers running exams, people structured in groups by age, following a curriculum—all of that. The whole system is based on a set of structural concepts that are incompatible with the presence of the computer. . . . But this will happen only in communities of children who have access to computers on a sufficient scale.* SEYMOUR PAPERT, 1984

> *Educational computing, like the Force, is with us. Microcomputers are proliferating in our schools and unless a lot of people are wrong they're here to stay. But the $64 question is whether these computers will make any difference in the education of our children. When my daughter graduates from high school in the year 2000, will she have received a better education with the help of computers than I did without them?* DALE PETERSON, 1984

In 1982 *Time* magazine put a computer on the cover of its issue heralding the editors' choice of "Man of the Year." In a special section headlined "Here Come the Microkids," *Time* added cutely that by "bits and bytes, the new generation spearheads an electronic revolution."[1] Predictions of the "information revolution" turn up in publication after publication. *Popular Computing* editors concluded that "schools are in the grip of a computer mania."[2] Surveys report on the growing number of desk-top computers purchased by school districts. An editorial in *InfoWorld* cautions us about "Fighting the School Computer Fad."[3] Computer summer camps for children pop up like daisies every May. Two year olds in preschool sit in front of terminals, feet dangling eight inches off the floor, and punch in commands to machines. Workshops where teachers learn to program and use classroom computers are common. In the midst of fiscal retrenchment, parents raise thousands of dollars to buy microcomputers for their children's schools. As with film, radio, and instructional television, predictions of computers reshaping how schools will be organized, how teachers will teach, and how students will learn surface repeatedly. The unrelenting search for ever greater classroom productivity continues.

The usual cycle of predicting extraordinary changes in teacher practice followed by academic studies of computers' classroom effectiveness, in turn followed by teacher reports about glitches in hardware, software, and logistics—all of this happened with computer-assisted instruction (CAI) almost two decades ago. With the advent of inexpensive desk-top machines and the promise of each student interacting with a personal computer, claims for a classroom revolution surfaced again.[4]

Yet how different is this current enthusiasm from the surge of interest in instructional television three decades ago or in classroom radio and motion pictures over a half century ago? The superficial similarities between periodic gushes in enthusiasm haunt conferences on educational technology like Marley's ghost. The similarities in claims, media interest, and investment are too vivid to simply brush aside as cynical mumblings from neanderthal educators.

But there is, of course, a danger in viewing everything as a passing fad; recognizing a permanent and dramatic shift in practice becomes almost impossible when the metaphor of a pendulum or cycle dominates the conventional view of change in public schools. The earthquake is a change metaphor also. Did people seeing their first locomotive, telephone, automobile, and television set know instantaneously that society's tectonic plates had shifted, jolting their lives forever? Will computers in schools have as much impact on what happens as these technological inventions have had in creating new patterns of living? No one can say with any conviction. "It's hard to predict," physicist Niels Bohr was supposed to have said,"especially the future."[5]

As aids in probing the present enthusiasm for classroom computers, I offer the following set of questions. The first three are drawn from research on the spread of other technological innovations. The final question is seldom asked by policy makers or researchers, yet it is fundamental to the making of school and classroom policy.[6]

1. What is the nature of the innovation?
2. How is it being introduced?
3. Who are the users, and how much are the machines used?
4. Should computers be used in classrooms?

WHAT IS THE NATURE OF THE INNOVATION?

Advocates and observers have noted frequently the uniqueness of the computer, both in supplementing and transforming conventional classroom content and skills. Computers can display an electronic chalkboard that students can use for practicing essential skills. According to promoters, computers can lead children into understanding how the mind works in solving a problem. The process of writing and debugging a program, for example, breaks down problems into smaller, manageable chunks. Awareness of both logical and procedural thinking grows. Furthermore, there is the powerful tug that the machine has in capturing student interest—the pinball effect. Hooking children into learning with computers, boosters claim, also gives them a growing sense of self-esteem, a feeling of competence, even control, especially when students can teach adults how to use the machines. This sense of control over the machine, the argument goes, is vital to children acting independently.

The versatility of the machine's uses for drill, problem solving, motivation, and interaction suggest differences of such a magnitude as to dwarf comparisons with earlier classroom technologies that usually possessed only one or two of these characteristics. Policy makers and practitioners alike are lured by the promise of finally achieving the engineer's dream of individual instruction through a machine that has the capacity to drill and tutor each student swiftly and cheaply without regard to the pace of classmates, while simultaneously recording and reporting achievement.

Like radio, film, and video, however, there are hardware and software issues. As prices for microcomputers fall, accessibility to these machines increases. Manufacturers and reformers dream of the day when every student will have a desk-top computer. Stunning jumps in school-district purchases and corporate gift programs suggest student access to machines will expand beyond the current handful of computers for each school. Nonetheless, the programs that run the machines continue to influence school use.[7] Inadequate software, especially in social studies, English, foreign languages, art, and music continues to weaken efforts to increase teacher use. Unsuitable programs persist since costs to produce improved software remain high. Even with these substantial issues, unquenched enthusiasm for computers in schools continues.[8]

HOW IS THE INNOVATION BEING INTRODUCED?

As with film, radio, and instructional television, cultural forces pressed schools to embrace computers. Growing concern for the United States losing its grip on markets that had U.S. stamped all over them (e.g., steel, autos, and high-tech industries) drove corporate officials to examine public schools and to join lawmakers in correcting what came to be viewed as a national problem: the inefficiency of U.S. schools in producing sufficient numbers of engineers, mathematicians, technicians, and workers flexible enough to survive in a rapidly changing workplace. Many states, for example, mandated stiffer graduation requirements, including a course in computer literacy.

Even before lawmakers wrote such language into bills, many parents, themselves touched by the computerization of the workplace, feared that their children lagged behind in college and job competition. Television commercials showed teachers suggesting to anxious parents the purchase of a home computer that would help their child do homework. Parents urged school boards to buy classroom computers. Active mothers and fathers went further and gave micro-computers to schools, a clear signal to the principal and teachers that the machines were to be used with children. Thus, much of the drumbeat for instructional use of computers came from outside schools.[9]

Not all administrators and teachers had to be drafted into the campaign for classroom use of the new machine. Substantial numbers of teachers promoted computers, and networks of computer buffs sprang up across the country. In visiting schools, for example, I frequently would meet at least one teacher or principal who believed deeply in the importance of students using computers. Championing the computer in that school or district, the practitioner and a small band of colleagues would lobby the central office for money and time to build a program. Sometimes inventive and entrepreneurial, such practitioners would beg foundations and local businesses for tax-sheltered gifts of micro-computers, just to launch a program. They appeared, however, to be the exceptions. Most teachers and administrators seemed initially to be uninvolved in the hoopla.[10]

Once under way in a school or district, though, a growing clamor from policy makers increased pressure upon teachers to enlist in the movement. Other teachers joined regular users who saw early the rising tide and wanted their students to be part of the apparent information revolution. Already, there are some discernible patterns emerging.

Computers turn up in classes of willing users or teachers who are asked by the principal to take a workshop so they can teach a new computer course the following year. More often than not, teachers who may have a home computer and have expressed interest or see the connection with their subject (frequently math and science) volunteer. Programs for gifted students turn up as common reasons for introducing computers into elementary schools, with the machines located in the library. There has been much variety in which schools (i.e., urban, suburban, or rural) adopted micro-computers, and how they did so. This again highlights the external push for accelerated use of the machine and the intense internal uncertainty over the best use of the new technology.[11]

Note how previous efforts to install new technologies into schools also encountered initial enthusiasm from many school boards, superintendents, and groups of teachers. In those instances, the decision to adopt classroom radio programs or video lessons came from the top of the organization. Implementation directives flowed downward; that is, plans were drawn, money appropriated, equipment purchased, and guidelines distributed from district head-quarters. The current embrace of the new computer technology, however, contains simultaneous top-down and bottom-up movement.[12]

Faced with uncertainty about computer use and the swift changes in the technology but still hearing a strong signal from parents and school boards to do something with computers, careful superintendents and principals, acting as gatekeepers for innovations entering their schools, have purchased some machines. For the principal, compliance with a school board's or superintendent's interest produces a few machines located in the library or the rooms of some teacher advocates. A few machines buy necessary insurance for withstanding criticism from parents and superiors for blocking the future. Such token adoption of an innovation, echoing earlier school responses to machines, not only insulates a principal (or superintendent) from static over the presence of modern technology in schools but also buffers unwilling or unconvinced teachers from the intrusive enthu-siasm of boosters. Hence, the number of machines in schools grows, feeding researchers' appetites for statistics on number of machines per building. As with other innovations, however, such figures seldom bear a strong relationship to the frequency of teacher or student use.

WHO ARE THE USERS, AND HOW MUCH
ARE THE MACHINES USED?

Teachers and administrators are the primary users. The computer's power to store, process, and retrieve information about attendance, scheduling, grades, inventories, and a host of other clerical tasks make it ideal for administrative uses both in the principal's office and the classroom. Other classroom uses fall into the visual workbook category, with simulations, writing, and machine tutoring among the less-used options. Teaching students to program computers appears to be increasing.

Elementary-school teachers use drill software in skill subjects, and the use of LOGO and programs for writing is reportedly growing. In secondary schools, the common pattern is to install a computer lab with twenty or more machines and schedule students for courses in programming or district-devised versions of computer literacy. Generally, math and science teachers use machines for classroom instruction more often than English, social studies, and foreign language teachers. Teachers, then, still control how much the classroom door opens to admit computers and how much they are used—provided, of course, that machines and appropriate software are accessible.[13]

The few statistics on classroom use underlines the uneven, limited penetration of machines into teachers' instructional repertoires. Determining what levels of teacher use now exist is like trying to snap a photograph of a speeding bicyclist. Every few months, a new survey on school computers announces increased purchases. One survey reports that the number of microcomputers available for instructional use tripled in 18 months (fall 1980 to spring 1982) to over 100,000 machines.[14] Two years later, that number climbed to 325,000. By 1984, of the 82,000 schools in the nation, 56,000 (or 68 percent) had at least one computer (either a terminal or micro), for an average of one machine for every 92 students.[15] In 1985, 92 percent of all secondary schools had at least one machine available for instruction; for elementary schools, it was 82 percent. The number of machines per school jumped sharply also. By 1984, the average elementary school had 5 machines, while the typical secondary school had just over 13.[16]

Such figures echo the results drawn from surveys on radio and television sets and film projectors. Although district purchases of equipment made machines accessible to schools, actual use of the earlier technologies by teachers and students was disappointing to promoters.

A 1981–1982 mid year survey of computer use, done by Johns Hopkins University researchers, calculated that almost 5 million students averaged nine hours each in front of a computer during the entire year. They reported that computers went unused more than half of the school day in three out of every four schools. Most schools used the computer (usually located in tightly secured labs, the library, math and science rooms, or the principal's office) about an hour a day. Student use varied between less than thirty minutes a week for three-quarters of lower-grade children to almost an hour a week for the same percentage of junior and senior high-school students.[17] Rand researchers studied sixty elementary- and secondary-school teachers identified as exemplary users of classroom computers in twenty-five California school districts. These regular and frequent users reported that students spent less than an hour a week receiving instruction via classroom computers.[18]

Even were those figures to double and triple in the next few years, it would still mean the typical elementary-school student would work a computer about 1.5 hours a week, while for upper-grade students the figure would be less than three hours a week. (Note that an instructional week typically runs between twenty-five to thirty hours.) None of these calculations, of course, considers how the curriculum would be reshaped to accommodate increased machine use, especially assuming that the amount of instructional time each week remains as it is. Nor do any of these calculations consider the differences in access to machines between male and female, white and nonwhite, and rich and poor students.[19]

And teacher use? In schools with computers, the Johns

Hopkins University study found that only one or two teachers regularly used them. Researchers also found that computer use depended upon where in the building the machines were put. A National Education Association (NEA) questionnaire of its membership in 1982 also reported infrequent use. Teacher interest in using the machines ran high, according to the NEA survey, but only 6 percent said that they used the machines in their classrooms. More than 80 percent said that they would like to take computer courses.[20]

Coming as they do in the beginning years of an enthusiasm of new technology aimed at altering classroom instruction, these surveys report a small but growing number of computers per building, limited student contact with the technology, few teachers with machines in their classrooms, and a growing cadre of energetic, willing colleagues using microcomputers as an adjunct to the core of instructional approaches.

Such results, again, echo familiar tones from earlier efforts to install innovations; however, patterns of infrequent film and video use were reported a decade or more after the technology was introduced, and microcomputers (excluding the twenty-year experience with CAI) are yet in their infancy. Low estimates of use may be due only to the common obstacles of inaccessible hardware, inappropriate software, and untrained teachers. I suspect, however, that, even if teacher use of machines and student contact triples, such levels of usage still would disappoint reformers and policy makers. Even then, most teachers still would be closing their doors to the technology, and the percentage of the instructional time each week devoted to desktop computers still would be slight. Were that to occur, I would expect that teachers, as in the past, would stand accused of resisting progress, of being neotroglodytes.

The temptation to blame teachers for the uneven penetration of computers into classrooms is, indeed, seductive. How infuriating it must be for true believers in the machine's liberating qualities and sheer productivity to find teachers blocking classroom doors, preventing the entry of this magical innovation, this panacea for the school's problems. If uncritical admirers of this electronic technology succumb to the temptation, they, like their forbears, will overlook the importance of settings in shaping instructional behavior. Limited teacher use of new technology may be due to organizational constraints built into classrooms and schools as workplaces.

Using one computer in the classroom as a student tutor, with a library of software available to the teacher, falls within well-known terrain: that is, the teacher uses the machine as a learning center for occasional student play when class members have completed their assigned work. Using the machine to drill a student in fractions or grammar or using it with proper software to enrich students' knowledge also falls well within the familiar. Such teaching practices resemble earlier uses of films, radio, and instructional television. Programming a microcomputer to reduce teachers' paperwork by preparing and marking tests, keeping attendance, and recording grades is also an appealing and certainly possible classroom use.

Gradually introducing computers into classrooms for such instructional and administrative tasks may succeed, since these limited uses respond to teacher-defined problems. Such solutions help teachers to cope with classroom issues. But for most teachers to instruct students in programming, to use the computer as a problem-solving tool, to learn procedural reasoning, and to encourage students to work alone with the machine in order to learn new content and skills violates what many informed observers and practitioners know to be the organizational realities. Transforming classroom practices through the computer stretch well beyond what many teachers view as possible, given the persistent imperatives tucked away in the DNA of classroom life.

That DNA is what I sketched out earlier as the implacable realities that policy makers institutionalized over a century ago: A teacher is required to face thirty or more students in a classroom for a set period of time, maintain order, and inspire the class to learn content and skills mandated by the community. Over the last century, teachers have adapted to this setting by generating a repertoire of practical methods that have come to be called teacher-centered instruction, classroom teaching, direct instruction, and so forth. School and classroom settings, as they have been and are presently organized, determine in large part the general direction that formal instruction takes.

Yet different models of teaching and learning with computers, suggested by Thomas Dwyer, Seymour Papert, and others, argue against this conventional version of teaching. In Dwyer's work with students in Pittsburgh, for example, he has constructed math settings where students control the technology and teachers act as "knowledgeable facilitators." Labs where teachers and students jointly become "discoverers of truths" permitted Dwyer to construct an environment where the new technology made learning math both natural and exhilarating. The customary classroom arrangement with the teacher in control gives way, according to Dwyer, to student-controlled computers and a world of experiences to be "lived in by both teacher and student." According to Dwyer, such labs do exist, but only in a small number of schools.[21]

Similarly, Seymour Papert's work in a few New York City schools where teachers have been trained to use fifteen or more machines with students suggests that at some future point the current teacher-student bond would be realigned into a mutual search for knowledge in real-life settings, finally bringing into focus the dreams of John Dewey.[22]

Left unsaid in their work with school districts is that while such arrangements are special, thus far they remain far outside the mainstream of public schooling. Most reports of school use of computers describe one or two machines in a classroom, or a room equipped with ten to twenty desk-top microcomputers where programming and literacy (however defined) are taught.

SHOULD COMPUTERS BE USED IN CLASSROOMS?

At this point, let me tilt the analysis slightly by questioning a basic assumption that thus far has directed the discussion of computers used for instruction. All of this analysis and speculation has assumed that the machine is a necessity and a boon to schooling. State and district policy makers, manufacturers, reformers, and most researchers seldom ask whether computers *should* be introduced into schools for instructional use. They ask only *how* computers should be used.

Because a machine can be used as a tutor, tool, or tutee or some creative mix of these, how it is used is uncertain. A computer can be programmed to teach subject matter and skills to students in CAI; it can be used by both teachers and administrators as a tool for keeping attendance, grades, inventories, and scheduling; it can be used by both teachers and students to create programs in which both machine and person learn from one another. Uncertain as to how the machine should be used, policy makers ask questions such as

1. Should we provide every student with access to a computer for a minimal time period, to insure some degree of literacy?
2. Should all students be exposed to programming languages? If so, which language? BASIC? LOGO? PASCAL?
3. Should we pursue CAI?
4. Should every school have ten to fifteen machines in a laboratory that is accessible to classes and individual students?
5. Should the number of machines differ for lower- and upper-grade schools?

Because no research evidence provides reliable guidelines and no consensus among professional educators yet exists for how machines should be used for instruction, such questions (and there are numerous others) have wildly different price tags attached to answers that experts offer to policy makers.[23]

In short, while the machine's versatility and promise for instruction exceeds the minuses of persistent hardware and software problems, knotty policy questions over how to computerize classrooms still puzzle decision makers. Few top officials, however, stop asking the "how" questions long enough to reach the more fundamental issue: *Should computers be used in classrooms?*

Such a "should" question seems pointless, even anachronistic, in the rising tide of unrestrained glee for classroom computers. But unless debate occurs about the conditions under which computers may be used, I suspect that scorching criticism will be leveled once again at teachers and principals for blocking yet another innovative technology aimed at making classrooms productive. Tardy as this debate may be, open discussion is essential, if for no other reason than to map out the intellectual terrain that practitioners and non-educators must negotiate in dealing with computers in schools. Until recently, few scholars and policy makers considered this basic question. As gatekeepers to classrooms, teachers do ask the question of themselves and their colleagues. "The order of our questions is important," Harriet Cuffaro writes. "If *how* is asked before *why*, we will be building a shaky foundation."[24]

To ask this question of any technology, but especially about microcomputers, is to reopen inquiry into what the purposes of instruction are, what should be taught, and how children learn. These are tough and troubling points with which few policy makers wish to wrestle. I offer here three points of argument regarding whether or not teachers should use computers as a central or even substantial part of classroom instruction:

1. Cost-effectiveness of computers used in instruction
2. Increased mechanization of teaching
3. Impact upon children

Cost-Effectiveness of Computers Used in Instruction

In all of the enthusiasm for classroom computers, an assumption that has gone largely unchallenged is that these machines, with appropriate programs, could teach students knowledge and skills both efficiently and effectively. The inference in the shadow of the assumption is that the new technology could get students to learn better, faster, and more cheaply than any other instructional tactic.

Economist Henry Levin and his associates partially tested that assumption and inference.[25] They chose four common tools policy makers use to improve math and reading skills: reducing class size, increasing the amount of time devoted to skill instruction, tutoring, and computer-assisted instruction. The researchers collected all the studies done on these strategies and statistically analyzed their findings, especially how much effect each intervention had on student performance as measured by test scores. They then priced what each component of the strategy would cost. Combining the known effects of each approach with its total costs, the researchers produced a cost-effectiveness ratio.[26]

What these researchers found is in some ways surprising. Students teaching students (peer tutoring) emerged as far more cost-effective than computer-assisted instruction. CAI was slightly more cost-effective than reducing class size from thirty-five to thirty or even to twenty students. Increasing the amount of time devoted to math and reading was by far the least cost effective.[27]

The researchers post a number of cautions about the study's limitations. For example, they used a popular CAI program concentrating on drill; other programs and computer uses might have been superior. Also, costs and results on an approach may vary in time from school to school.[28]

Aware of the study's limitations, I only note this research as simply one instance of applying two criteria favored by so many policy makers: efficiency and effectiveness. My point is not to convince anyone that hiring older students to coach younger ones is cheaper and better than stocking a lab with desk-top computers. Rather, I wish to underscore the flabbiness in the assumption that computerized instruction is automatically superior to other conventional classroom approaches in boosting academic performance. New machines stocked with flawless software may hook students' interest and improve their proficiencies, but the unit costs may be prohibitive compared to alternatives. Computerized instruction used as a tool, tutor, or tutee should not escape application of this criterion.

Increased Mechanization of Teaching

Converting teaching into a science historically has driven many reformers, researchers, and policy makers toward embracing numerous innovations that have promised precision harnessed to efficiency. Raymond Callahan documented how academics and administrators in the early decades of this century seized upon scientific management as both a philosophy and set of tools with which to transform American schools into productive businesses. The marriage of efficiency experts and educational administrators produced by the 1920s a mindset among scholars and practitioners that schools could be managed like corporations.[29]

Viewing schools as bureaucracies and teachers as technicians who execute in their classrooms mandates ordered by top-level managers is a perspective that has ebbed and flowed in popularity since the 1920s. Efforts to introduce systematic classroom procedures and rational teaching methods became especially faddish in the 1960s and 1970s with the growing awareness on the part of state and federal policy makers that many American children left school unfit to read, write, and calculate.

The surge of popular interest in making schools productive and accountable spurred efforts to train teachers to write precise objectives aimed at producing student results (e.g., "by June, 95 percent of my class will list correctly and in chronological order the wars that America fought since 1776"). Many teacher education institutions altered their curricula by breaking down the act of teaching into measurable behaviors that could be taught separately to prospective teachers (e.g., how to praise students, how to ask questions). States mandated testing programs that required teachers to concentrate on the skills that legislators believed were important (e.g., minimum competency tests, reading and math achievement exams). More recently, the Effective Schools reform movement, which gives special attention to improving low-income, minority students' test scores through a variety of school-based and district-directed strategies, has focused on certain teaching methods (e.g., monitoring student

Now Apple makes it easy to become attached to your students.

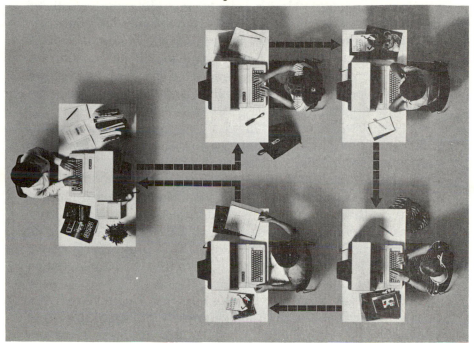

Introducing the Apple® SchoolBus™ network. A complete cable, interface, and software package that connects your teacher's station to as many as 30 students' computers.

So much for the technical explanation.

Because what it really does is allow you to realize the full potential of the complete computer classroom.

By helping to make you a more effective teacher. By allowing you to communicate with your students as never before.

And by doing it all at 20% less than the cost of individual standalone systems.

With the SchoolBus network in place, you'll be able to view any student's work — at any time — from your own station.

So you can see how well they're doing, even while they're doing it.

You can also exchange messages, suggest changes, or offer encouragement for a job well done.

Having this kind of capability (the kind that lets you be in more than one place at one time) is perfect for the programming lab, where the lesson is built line by line.

But SchoolBus can also be used to teach anything.

And make it easier than ever for everyone.

With SchoolBus, you can restrict student access to certain files. Like other students' files. Or your own.

And it also has a password capability to maintain the privacy of each student.

Student access to disk drives, printers, and software is also controlled by you. So you can tell your students exactly when and where to get on and off the system, and students never have to handle disks themselves.

SchoolBus is much more economical than individual standalone systems, because you don't have to buy disk drives for everyone in the room. The same goes for printers.

And software. Since there's no need for anyone but you to have a program.

The savings can be as much as a third of the entire system cost.

What's more, the SchoolBus works with any of the Apple II family of systems.

The SchoolBus network is just part of Apple's Complete Classroom, including all the hardware you'll ever need, and more educational software than is available for any other personal computer.

One of our 1500 authorized Apple dealers can tell you more.

Just tell them you'd like to do some homework on the SchoolBus.

They'll know what you mean.

Soon there'll be just two kinds of people. Those who use computers and those who use Apples.

Call **(800) 538-9696** for the location of the authorized Apple dealer nearest you, or for information regarding our National Account Program. In Canada, call **(800) 268-7796** or **(800) 268-7637**. Or write Apple Computer Inc., Advertising and Promotion Dept., 20525 Mariani Ave., Cupertino, CA 95014. © 1983 Apple Computer Inc.

Courtesy Apple Computer, Inc.

work, clarity in presenting information, question asking).
Research has shown that these instructional practices yield
improved test scores. Central to all of these efforts is the
impulse to make teaching planned, systematic, and
engineered.[30]

These and other developments, including the growth of
unions and collective bargaining, have hardened the view
that schools and classrooms are places where complex tasks
can be broken apart, improved, and put back together to
produce informed and skilled graduates. Teaching, according
to this perspective, can be done by anyone who possesses the
appropriate technical skills.

The periodic surges of interest in introducing video, film,
radio, and computers overlap these larger efforts to bureau-
cratize schooling and rationalize teaching. Promoters believe
that these machines give teachers additional tools for
enhancing productivity. The unexamined assumption, of
course, is that policy makers committed to viewing instruction as a technical process believe that student learning is
mechanical; that is, what teachers do skillfully will cause
predictable student outcomes. No persuasive body of evidence
exists yet to confirm that belief.

Few of the various reform efforts have considered seriously the crucial nonrational elements of teaching. Some
reseachers have pointed out how highly teachers prize the
emotional bonds with students, bonds that nourish learning.
Others have found that teachers see student academic and
emotional growth in holistic rather than narrow, fragmented
terms. A few researchers have written how teachers see what
they do as much closer to an art than a science. Affection for
speed, accuracy, detail, and efficiency—benchmarks for the
engineer—are respected and at times even cultivated by
teachers but clearly are of secondary importance to classroom
learning. Such views embedded in how teachers see what
they do slow the conversion of teaching into a technical
process.[31]

Too often forgotten by policy makers intent upon transforming teaching practice is how much classroom learning is
anchored in the emotional lives of thirty children and one

teacher together for large chunks of time in a small, crowded space. What some have labeled "emotional rationality" only underlines how divorcing the mind from feelings and the senses robs children of learning about drama, music, art, nature, and relationships with responsible, caring adults. Even in the hard-core, cognitive skills of analysis, emotions fuel the drive for understanding and soften the abrasive edge of calculation.[32]

The complex relationships between teachers and students become uncertain in the face of microcomputers. What holds many teachers in classrooms for large portions of their life-times are the inner pleasures gained from contacts with young people. The keen satisfaction that comes from seeing an able student mature intellectually and emotionally rewards a teacher, regardless of whether the student or parent acknowledges the teacher's contribution. Teachers gain pleasure from the emotional circuitry wired into intense bonds that develop between them and certain students, often lasting for decades. The touches, smiles, warmth, and even the frowns, annoyance, and anger that pass between teacher and student cement ties that deepen learning and give gratification to teachers.[33]

I mean to portray no rhapsodic Winslow Homer scene of silver-haired teachers and laughing students alive to one another and their surroundings threatened by the golem of computerized learning. I mean only to say the obvious: Classrooms are steeped in emotions. In the fervent quest for precise rationality and technical efficiency, introducing to each classroom enough computers to tutor and drill children can dry up that emotional life, resulting in withered and uncertain relationships.

Students working with computers alone or in pairs for long periods of time lose time for direct and sustained contact with teachers. Bonds develop instead between students and machines. Information comes from the machine; the machine generates praise and nudges the student along programmed paths constructed to guide the user to further learning. Adult-child ties may unravel as a consequence of the newly developed child-machine liaison.[34]

While the argument can be carried to an extreme, making the classroom into a setting where few exchanges occur, that is not my intention. Some enthusiasts even argue that machines *increase* student-teacher interaction. The point I offer is simply that those advocates who push for a shift in the control of learning from teachers to students interacting with machines probably misunderstand how teacher communication, expectations, and feelings produce those very classroom features that give a human touch to instruction and generate those intense inner pleasures for teachers. Because so much of teaching is imagination, improvisation, and pacing combined with student rapport, shifting the center of gravity to machine-student exchanges lessens greatly the joys inherent to the art of teaching. At a deep level that often goes unspoken, I believe that many teachers may sense how the introduction of machines into classrooms endangers those intangible, highly prized rewards that count so heavily in why teachers decide to endure in a most difficult but intensely satisfying job.

These issues surely play a role in why the mechanization of teaching has proceeded so slowly over the last century. Efforts to introduce behavorial objectives, competency-based teacher education, and technology were seldom wholly or even partially successful in transforming classrooms into squeakless, efficient operations tended by teacher-mechanics. While there is much in classrooms that appears mechanical, such as lesson plans, rows of desks, worksheets, and textbook assignments, these practices do not constitute the core experiences or central aspects of most classroom life.

The major resistance to converting classrooms into technical enterprises, as I suggested, has come from the organizational realities of school and classroom life and the teacher's holistic perspective on what's important to young people. Without knowing exactly what the anticipated—much less the unanticipated—consequences of shipping machines into classrooms will be, prudence would suggest a yellow flashing light rather than a green one. Beyond whispering caution in policy makers' ears, however, here are some thoughts:

- Maybe the teacher's perspective about learning and children is correct. Perhaps learning is largely opportunistic, spontaneous, and unpredictable. In classrooms with a couple of desk-top computers, teachers and students still can take advantage of those special moments. But computer-rich classrooms geared to machine-student interactions are very different settings that construct a very different role for the teacher.
- Maybe the pedagogy (large- and small-group instruction, discussions, seatwork, textbook assignments, and so on) that teachers hold with great persistence (and that reformers label as archaic and inefficient) should be bolstered and improved upon. That pedagogy still provides an emotional foundation to cognitive growth and may need to be nourished, enhanced, and protected, but not satirized.

In a culture in love with swift change and big profit margins, yet reluctant to contain powerful social mechanisms that strongly influence children (e.g., television), no other public institution offers these basic but taken-for-granted occasions for continuous, measured intellectual and emotional growth of children. Without much evidence to support unrestrained entry of machines into classrooms, reopening policy discussions on both the *how* and the *why* seem to be in order. In that renewed policy discussion, both the merits of computers as classroom tools and the qualitative issues embedded in the act of teaching need to be considered seriously, especially because teaching is less susceptible to measurement but so profoundly important to the subjective, artistic side of instruction. As Philip Jackson says:

> People who are interested in the application of learning theory or the engineering point of view to teaching practice often have as their goal the transformation of teaching from something crudely resembling an art to something crudely resembling a science. But there is no good evidence to suggest that such a transformation is either possible or desirable. An equally reasonable goal ... is to seek an understanding of the teaching process as it is commonly

performed before making an effort to change it. As we learn more about what goes on in these densely populated hives of educational activity it may turn out that we will seek to preserve, rather than to transform, whatever amount of artistry is contained in the teacher's work.[35]

Impact on Children

If the full influence, both positive and negative, of television watching on children continues to be debated three decades after its introduction, how can anyone assess the complexity of what happens to children using classroom computers? The image of five year olds pressing keys to create designs on a screen or learning to write or solve a problem feeds the enthusiasm of many parents and educators. But no one can answer with confidence the question of what impact continuous exposure to the surrogate reality called up on a computer screen has upon children.

All we see in the media are the attractive, eye-catching pictures of small children working with machines. Concerns seldom are raised about negative or questionable influences. My concerns at this time concentrate on these three points:

1. No consensus exists among scholars and practitioners on how children should learn and how teachers should teach.
2. There is much uncertainty over what students can learn from computerized lessons.
3. Collateral learning may be more significant in children's lives than the formal lessons taught by machines.

Lack of Consensus on Learning Theories and Teaching Methods

Among teachers, administrators, and researchers, various theories of learning compete for attention. Operant conditioning, information processing, and social learning are three dominant ways of viewing how children learn. While practitioner vocabulary is often atheoretical (as in most practical arts), conceptual frameworks drawn from one or more of these theories exist in their minds, nonetheless. Teacher beliefs, for example, are working theoretical models that guide decision making regarding how to present content, how to teach skills, how to build student confidence, and a dozen other "hows" of teaching. Although few teachers would use the technical language favored by researchers, the basic core of concepts within each theory is familiar.

To cope with the awesome complexity of diversity in students and the unexpected in classroom life, practitioners develop expert knowledge of situations that arise in classes. In identifying any single learning episode, the experienced teacher chooses a strategy that fits the demands of that particular situation, tailoring instructional tactics to match the situation's inevitable uniqueness. What teachers select from their expert knowledge and apply to the singular setting is anchored in one or more theoretical constructs. No single theory of learning (or instruction) yet encompasses the uniqueness of classroom events or student differences.[36]

Computerized learning, however, is anchored in at least two of these theories: operant conditioning (drill) and information processing (programming). Teachers will use software that gets students to practice skills or remember knowledge—staples of teaching practice. Drill is common and considered by teachers as an important, if not tedious, instructional task. Already such software accounts for a substantial portion of machine use in classrooms. I see no problem here.

Where I see a potential issue is the growing popularity of LOGO, BASIC, and other programming languages. Formal languages appeal to advocates of classroom machines because they believe that children learning to program will develop analytic thinking skills and procedural reasoning that goes far beyond what teachers do in classrooms now. Drawing turtles and geometric figures on the screen and assembling programs, for example, teaches students to be aware of how both the machine and the human mind operate as information processors. The accelerating passion for LOGO as a means for teaching preschoolers to read and write accepts implicitly a cognitive learning theory that dwells upon such concepts as attention, memory, and retrieval of information. Both theoretical and practical questions arise from this constricted view of a growing child as an information processor.[37]

Adherents of the theories of Jean Piaget (including computer scientist Seymour Papert) stress the various developmental stages of thought that children pass through. But computer enthusiasts who advocate giving children a head start by getting them to think abstractly as soon as possible argue that seven year olds can leapfrog a developmental phase; that is, they can move from preoperational (ages 2–7) to formal operations (ages 11–16) without passing through concrete operating (ages 7–11). Critics suggest that this is a misreading of Piaget and is, at best, experimental. At worst, such a view perpetuates a narrow view of children as mere collections of cognitive abilities divorced from feeling and contact with stimulating surroundings.[38]

Furthermore, there is simply no persuasive body of evidence that children learning how to think procedurally or conceptually can transfer that learning to other settings. In a stinging rebuke of the notion of transfer, another computer scientist, Joseph Weizenbaum, responded this way to an interviewer's query about how computers improve children's problem-solving abilities: "If that were true, then computer professionals would lead better lives than the rest of the population. We know very well that isn't the case. There is, as far as I know, no more evidence programming is good for the mind than Latin is, as is sometimes claimed."[39]

The major point is that a heavy reliance upon classroom computers would draw heavily upon cognitive learning theory alone, forcibly narrowing teachers' repertoires enough to diminish the range of approaches skilled practitioners could use in classrooms. Moreover, such emphasis upon machines would be a terribly risky experiment, because researchers lack sufficient evidence that children exposed to machine interaction for long periods of time develop the full range of values, knowledge, and skills expected by parents and the community. Just because researchers and visionary academics see computers as an inexorable tide engulfing this society is not sufficient justification for experimenting upon a captive and naive population.

What Can Students Learn from Computerized Lessons?

The claims that students acquire basic skills through CAI have been verified over the last two decades. CAI is effective in certain domains, under certain conditions. Whether it is cost-effective or enhances other instructional goals, of course, are separate and contestable issues.

Some claim that computers also will teach students more powerful ways of thinking than presently are taught. In the last section I mentioned the criticism of this assertion: beyond assertions and rebuttals, however, few studies have produced consistent findings that support either side of the exchange. Caution in purchasing equipment and software for this purpose seems appropriate, given the uncertainty, in both research and practice, over the quality and effectiveness of what is learned from computers.[40]

What Kinds of Learning Are Most Important to Children?

"Perhaps the greatest of all pedagogical fallacies," John Dewey wrote in *Experience and Education*, "is the notion that a person learns only the particular thing he is studying at the time."[41] Collateral learning—absorption of attitudes that accompany the formal lesson—often exceeds the importance of what is taught directly.

No body of evidence on collateral learning yet exists to persuade critics or advocates of classroom computers how much more is learned by students beyond the lesson on the screen. I include this point because such learning is observable, but its magnitude, pervasiveness, and persistence remain open to questions.

Harriet Cuffaro asks what a youngster learns when she presses the keyboard to call up cars and garages on a screen to figure out how to park a car in the garage. Eye-hand coordination? Perhaps. A sense of control? Not really, since the programmed instructions produce alternate paths from which the child chooses. She directs the car on the screen, unaware of the mysterious program as she presses the keys. Cuffaro than asks what occurs when the same girl parks a car when playing with blocks. Her eye-hand coordination now must deal with three dimensions, not just the two on the screen. The block that is the car must be maneuvered physically, by hand, to fit into a garage made of blocks. Cuffaro says, "The computer version of parking a car is action in a vacuum, motion without context, and with reality twice removed."[42]

She argues that the unanticipated lessons that children pick up informally when working with microcomputers should give educators pause before plunging ahead with the new technology.

> It is the presence of these collateral learnings—the distance and narrowing of physical reality, the magical quality of pressing keys, the "invisible" sharing of control, the oversimplification of process, the need for precision and timing—that merit great attention when thinking about young children's learning and the use of microcomputers.[43]

Cuffaro and others single out the computer's power to teach many significant, misleading, and unintentional lessons to children beyond the programmed ones. Few researchers can say with much confidence what the effect is, upon any given child, of sustained exposure to a two-dimensional reality displayed on a computer screen. Few scholars have investigated the computer learning environment, which John Davy calls "mentally rich" but "perceptually extremely impoverished."[44]

Even fewer researchers know what attitudes children carry away from prolonged contact with computerized lessons. Davy suggests in his critique of *Mindstorms* that if this technology is needed to introduce children to powerful ideas because teachers can't, as Seymour Papert argues, what does that teach children about where ideas come from? What, Davy asks rhetorically, is more cognitively powerful than people? If teachers do an inept job of presenting and generating ideas, "should we not be looking at how teachers work rather than selling them a prosthesis?"[45]

Skeptics like Davy make a fundamental point in their criticism of massive classroom use of computers:

> At the heart of real life is working with people, being with people, understanding people. . . . As long as classrooms include real teachers, cognitive development cannot, in the nature of the situation, be divorced from emotional, social, and moral experience.[46]

Joseph Weizenbaum makes a similar point from a different angle. Because the programmer's thinking is linear, logical, and rule governed, that kind of technical, analytic thought (highly prized by engineers and policy makers) magnifies what he calls "instrumental reasoning." Such reasoning amplifies calculation, prizes numbers, and elevates scientific experts to social engineers; such reasoning, he says, has little to do with creativity, intuition, and feeling.[47]

What, then, is learned from computers? Davy, Weizenbaum, and others claim that computerized reasoning is essentially technical and nonemotional, divorced from the richness of human experience. The brain's cortex is not a whole human being; it is an important part but still a fragment. Computerized reasoning is but a sliver of the emotional rationality that constitutes thought. For students to view what they get out of machines as equivalent to human thought, the critics assert, is both inaccurate and, ultimately, dangerous.

Another collateral learning is the child-machine relationship. Media report stories about robot-child friendships and the personalizing of machines, such as with mechanical voices telling car owners to close the door. Art Buchwald's one-liner, "being a computer means never having to say you're sorry," underscores the uneasy ambiguity over what machines are.[48] Sherry Turkle's *Second Self* also explores this gray area in a six-year study of emerging computer culture, including children in a private school where "every child had almost unlimited access to personal computers." In this and other computer-rich elementary schools—unlike most public schools now—she found that child programmers saw "machines as 'sort of' alive because in these cultures it became taboo to kill them, to 'crash' them, to interrupt programs running on them."[49]

Turkle also found that, in young children, teenagers, and college students, interacting with machines generated varied notions of human-ness and machine-ness. Some students came to see themselves as machines, both as a working model and as "protection from feeling, invulnerability to the threat of being swallowed up."[50] But one can also turn to the machine for relationships. Turkle describes the school's computer culture and Henry, the awkward, rude and withdrawn boy at the private school who relaxed in front of the computer. Here he was in control, forging a relationship that meant a lot to him.[51]

I am uncertain what lessons to draw for public schools from computer-rich private schools and video game arcades. Turkle's plumbing of the computer culture does raise basic issues about what else is learned, beyond programming by hooked students. Such issues touch the very core of what the human mind is and what the dimensions are of child-machine bonds. I would like to see more policy makers attending to these subtle but profound issues, even though it means addressing difficult questions and challenging the popularity of classroom computers.

Summary

To what degree, then, and under what conditions—if at all—should computers be used in classrooms? The arguments presented here have raised questions about cost-effectiveness, further mechanization of teaching, and impact upon children if substantial numbers of classroom computers entered classrooms.

To question computer use in schools is to ask what schools are for, why teachers teach certain content, how they should teach, and how children learn. Unsettling questions as these probe the uneasy silence in public debate over the new technology's use in classrooms, a silence that helps no one who is truly concerned over the schooling offered to the next generation.

I fear, however, that basic questions such as these will go unasked and unanswered because researchers, reformers, and policy makers will discover how little teachers use the machines. I predict that most teachers will use computers as an aid, not unlike radio, film, and television. In elementary schools where favorable conditions exist, teacher use will increase but seldom exceed more than 10 percent of weekly instructional time. Pulling out students for a 30-to-45-minute period in a computer lab will, I suspect, gain increasing popularity in these schools. Where unfavorable conditions exist (i.e., limited principal and central office support, few machines, and so forth), teachers who are serious computer users will secure machines but schoolwide use will be spotty. In secondary schools, the dominant pattern of use will be to schedule students into one or more elective (rather than required) classes where a score of desk-top computers sit. Computer buffs on the staff will develop classroom schemes for using machines in instruction. In no event would I expect general student use of computers in secondary schools to exceed 5 percent of the weekly time set aside for instruction. I predict no great breakthrough in teacher use patterns at either level of schooling. The new technology, like its predecessors, will be tailored to fit the teacher's perspective and the tight contours of school and classroom settings.

If this is what will occur, and based upon my research and experience, I believe that it will, then the common complaints about educator conservatism, stubborn teachers, stifling bureaucracies, and so forth will surface again. The blinders that nonteachers wear once again will shut out any awareness of the teacher's universe and the substantial impact that existing organizational arrangements in schools and classrooms have upon how teachers teach. Teachers, again, will receive rebukes for closing the classroom door to the magic of another technology. Debates over whether computers should be used in classrooms, under what conditions, and to what degree—if at all—will be buried in the scorn heaped upon intransigent teachers.

Sadly, few teachers, principals, superintendents, and school boards raise important points about cost-effectiveness of computerized instruction, nourishing the artistry of teachers, and buffering the classroom from insistent efforts to make instruction mechanical. Nor do many educators acknowledge openly the emotional content of classrooms and question the narrow band of rationality prized in computer learning, or ask about what else is learned by students when they master LOGO and other languages. Because few educators raise these or similar questions or call attention to the powerful behavioral influences of the settings within which they work, nonteachers easily conclude that the problems of increasing the number of desk-top machines is one solely of technical implementation—get the hardware, develop the software, train the teachers, and shove those machines past that classroom door. But the issue of computers for instruction is far more complex, going to the very core of the purposes of schooling.

Thus, my answer whether or not computers *should* be used in classrooms is a cautious one. Given the current organizational settings, classroom computers should be used by teachers to cope with the routine, often tedious, student learning problems that machines can do patiently. Such use is neither sinister nor wasteful, as some computer boosters suggest. Such use meets a teacher-defined problem well. As unimaginative as drill, simulations, games, and enrichment software may strike reformers, these uses do fit well teachers' needs in adapting to the restless, unpredictable nature of classroom life.

These restricted uses of the new technology appear outrageously conventional. Yet unless existing classroom and school settings are altered substantially, much beyond the conventional will be tough to attain. No computer advocates that I have read or heard, for example, have suggested that schools should hire more teachers and adults to reduce the teaching load, bringing it closer to the college schedule than to the factory. No computer advocate urges increasing school district budgets by half to modify the existing school and classroom arrangements concerning class size, governance, training, and teacher collaboration. Their sole recommendation is to put money into classroom computers.[52]

Until there is far more research, far more public debate among academics, policy makers, and practitioners about why teachers teach the way they do; about the linkages between resources and classroom settings; and about the consequences of computer-rich schools, I would urge moratoria on more teaching of technical languages to students and heavy purchasing of interactive computers. Too many complex, interrelated policy issues about the teacher's role, the act of teaching, collateral learning for students, and the purposes of schooling arise to press forward without questioning or anticipating consequences.

I will end this discussion by drawing a comparison to another public policy issue where a technological solution to a social problem went unexamined, the human consequences of which can be seen daily on city streets across America. In the 1950s and 1960s, the mentally ill were housed in institutions costing hundreds of millions of tax dollars. Researchers had begun to produce tranquilizers and other drugs that were billed as cures for psychoses, promising a revolution in the care of those in state institutions. Nationally, psychiatrists, researchers, political reformers, foundation executives, and professional organizations backed a policy of releasing the mentally ill from state facilities and letting community-based clinics handle them on an out patient basis, using the new miracle drugs. Studies that showed how well-staffed local clinics using drugs could treat patients in a much shorter time than state hospitals were used as ammunition by public officials anxious to shift heavy expenditures from state hospitals to other public ventures.

State after state legislated the release of mentally ill throughout the 1960s and 1970s. Federal legislation establishing community mental health centers spurred what came to be called the policy of de-institutionalization. What soon became apparent to many policy makers and local officials was that many severely ill patients had no business being released; drugs were insufficient to cope with many psychoses; and community health centers were inadequately staffed for dealing with schizophrenics and other psychotic clients. The sharp increase in homeless "street people" is simply one unanticipated consequence of the policy changes. Another is the long-term, undesirable effects of persistent drug use. The wholesale release of patients from state hospitals is generally regarded now as a failure in public policy.[53]

A former director of the National Institute of Mental Health and an advocate of this policy change recently thought back on those years:

> Many of those patients who left state hospitals never should have done so. We psychiatrists saw too much of the old snake pit, saw too many people who shouldn't have been there and we overreacted. The result is not what we intended, and perhaps we didn't ask the questions that should have been asked when developing a new concept, but psychiatrists are human, too, and we tried our damndest.[54]

Other policy makers and reformers thought about how they "oversold community treatment" and how "the professional community made mistakes and was overly optimistic, but the political community wanted to save money." Over-promising the benefits of drugs and the capacities of community health centers emerges as the theme of the reflections of both academics and policy makers.[55]

I offer this example of a policy anchored in advances in medical technology, fueled by an impulse toward making public institutions more productive, and fed by a political hunger to save tax dollars to suggest only the seriousness of prematurely pushing a policy change that has potentially grave human consequences. The push for classroom computers is certainly not as dramatic or as wrenching as what happened to hospital patients sent to communities unprepared to deal with them, but the unexamined assumptions, unasked questions, and overselling bear much similarity to the present situation. In dealing with lives, young or old, patience and public reflection on both the anticipated and unanticipated consequences of policies are in order, rather than the headlong plunge into change followed by a heartfelt apology years later.

Epilogue

I began this book with the example of a 1927 photograph of a Los Angeles teacher lecturing a class of seven aboard an airplane during an aerial lesson on geography. I used the photograph to identify the paradox of change amidst stability. In bringing this examination of technology and teaching practice to a close, I end with a few words on the paradox itself.

Few informed observers casting a careful, century-long look at schools could be blind to the changes that have occurred in public schools. Governance, curricula, and school organization, for example, have changed substantially since the closing decades of the nineteenth century. When observing changes in the classroom itself, however, there seem to have been only some modest alterations in classroom organization (more diversity in forms), teacher-student relationships (less formal), and instructional methods (a broader repertoire). What can hardly escape notice is the persistent core of practices that teachers have found to be efficient and resilient, engineered to fit the physics of the classroom. Thus, while governance, curricula, and organization have altered the district and school terrain sufficiently to be readily observed, shifts over the last century in classroom topography barely can be detected.

In effect, district and school organizations apparently have responded to external pressures for change in lumbering, erratic, and unanticipated ways. Nestled within the larger district and school contexts, yet insulated from the clamor for change, teachers also have responded to the insistent drumbeat for change in muted ways well fitted to the nature of classroom life. Because many reformers view the pace of district and school change as no swifter than a snail riding a turtle, schools have acquired the reputation for being backwater institutions reluctant to alter anything.

Part of the mislabeling problem is that reformers and policy makers have far more access to media and have fastened upon schools a narrow definition of the word "change." Policy makers and reformers looking for change ask only whether or not the adopted decisions were implemented as planned in schools and classrooms. If what happened in schools seems clearly linked to what was intended, then they believe that *real* change occurred. To the degree that a gap between intention and outcome appears, the cloud of failure arises, triggering the blaming process. All of this is to say that planned change is merely a subset of a broader definition of change—organizational adaptability.

Planners and academics interested in school improvement have dominated the literature on change and drafted a far narrower version of the word in the battle for reform. Intentional change (i.e., reform efforts, designs for improvement) is a small part of the larger process by which schools adapt to new information, external pressures, and dozens of other unplanned events. To telescope the broader meaning of change into the narrower one sloughs off the historical evidence of how schools have adapted over the last century by altering programs, governance, and beliefs. By ignoring data on adaptability, reformers misrepresent both the promise and limits of what can occur in public schools. Need I add that such a mish-mash in terms influences considerably how one views stability and change in schools. To press this point one step further, I will focus on two issues; (1) the importance of a sense of time and (2) the classroom as a workplace.[1]

With regard to time, too few educational researchers study phenomena for very long. In research designs, experimental groups may receive treatments ranging from an hour to a week, perhaps a month—seldom longer. Longitudinal studies of a decade or more are rare. The research literature displays abundant instances where investigators pronounced that an innovation, a program, or direction undertaken by a school or district had failed. The conclusion comes after studying the planned change for six months, a year, or perhaps two. No doubt there are excellent reasons for this impatience, including research costs and pressures to produce publications. But to historians, paleontologists, anthropologists, and other scientists, such impatience, while understandable, erodes the credibility of educational researchers' findings. Scientists who study humans and animals, for example, understand that decades, centuries, and even millenia may need to pass before some changes to become noticeable.

In reviewing the literature on schools and classrooms over the past century, changes, both intended and unintended, can be detected. These changes occur as a result of stable processes of change, ways that schools and classroom teachers respond to their environments. Only a tiny part of these changes are the designs of policy makers.[2]

Districts, individual schools, and classroom teachers all have ways of detecting problems in their surroundings, techniques of learning from experience, and tactics for constructing solutions to problems. Early warning systems, for example, are embedded in procedures that many school boards follow in listening to parents at public meetings, superintendents holding open doors, periodic surveys of citizen opinion, and so forth. Routines for learning from experience often are buried in standard operating procedures. School district policy manuals collect lessons learned from trial and error and offer these procedures as guides for daily decision making. Mistakes that crop up produce revisions in procedures. Negotiating solutions to conflict is a common practice among administrators and teachers, as, for example, in collective bargaining, appeal processes, and other routine responses to conflict. Over time, these routines tucked away in formal policies and the memories of veteran staff produce change.

Time, then, is crucial in identifying the enduring devices that organizations have constructed for responding to external demands for swift change. Stability and change are interwoven into a seamless cloth difficult for the observer to disentangle at first glance, yet becoming more visible as time passes.

In relation to this concept of time, reconsider the issue of computers in schools. The stable processes of change just noted also come into play here, as districts, schools, and individual teachers respond to insistent pressures that more desk-top computers be used for instruction. It is a safe bet that the degree that most districts and schools will incorporate machines into the administrative and instructional procedures will fall short of the dreams of manufacturers and enthusiastic policy makers. Yet at some level of adaptation, computers will appear in schools and be used in classrooms. If history is any guide, that incremental change—infinitesimal to the reformer's critical eye—will be a stable, attenuated response to the external challenge. The value of the modest change and its contribution to the effectiveness of instruction, are issues that require different questions beyond the simple one of what magnitude of change occurred. I raised such questions in the last chapter.

From the perspective of the reformer, such a muted response to computers could be labeled as another failure of technology, another improvement blocked by teachers. From the perspective of veteran practitioners and policy makers, wise to the complexities of social institutions and modest in aspirations, such slow and marginal changes appear as substantial, given the conflicting goals, limited resources, and organizational settings that constrain classrooms. Thus, change may well be in the beholder's eye. After a storm has struck a beach, to get down on your hands and knees and look at the sand from an inch away will give a clear but limited view of the beach; it will not offer a whole picture of what the storm has done to the shoreline.

Consider now the importance of classrooms as workplaces. The issues teachers face daily are anchored in the very nature of compulsory schooling and the organizational settings that have been constructed in response to the demands for mass schooling. As part of their occupational culture, teachers have built informal criteria for what will and won't work in their classrooms. These criteria by which teachers judge what is productive are embedded in an ethic of practicality. Craft wisdom, lore, experience-based repertoires, and formal policies buttress these criteria. While teacher responses change over time as their beliefs alter and as they react to different surroundings, marginal alterations in practice can be identified over time.

To those interested in planned change, patience and understanding seem to be essential. Patience is needed for accepting that what is intended seldom materializes immediately, and understanding is required for working with the stable processes of change at work in districts, schools, and classrooms. Historically, reformers intent upon modifying teaching practices have been driven far more by dreams of school improvements that will address larger social problems and much less by any sensitive awareness of what teachers need to do in order to alter what happens in classrooms.

With so much written about change and its consequences, I find it striking that fundamental propositions about change, easily shared by most informed observers and professionals, remain in the shadows, even amidst periodic surges of fervor for designing changes. In the years following World War II, anthropologist Edward Spicer and a number of colleagues studied the impact of change upon varied cultures. They collected a number of case studies of preindustrial and industrial cultures coming to grips with change. In *Human Problems in Technological Change* he extracted from these and other studies a series of statements that today sound like clichés:

- People resist changes that appear to threaten basic securities.
- People resist proposed changes they do not understand.
- People resist being forced to change.
- Changes generated in one subculture where science and technology are highly valued, if they are to be accepted in another subculture, must be made understandable and given clear value.[3]

These generalizations produce little disagreement among policy makers and well-intentioned reformers. Yet, as Harry

Wolcott has observed, "the lessons are *recited* rather than *learned*" (italics in original).[4]

This study illustrates that the search for improving classroom productivity through technological innovations has yielded very modest changes in teacher practice without any clear demonstration that instruction is any more effective or productive after the introduction of radio, films, instructional television, or computers. Implicit in this history is that policy makers determined to modify classroom practice need to be well informed. They need to understand clearly that what gives stability to teaching is a classroom universe tightly coupled to organizational settings. Teacher repertoires, both resilient and efficient, have been shaped by the crucible of experience and the culture of teaching. Policy makers need to understand that altering pedagogy requires a change in what teachers believe. Getting professionals to unlearn in order to learn, while certainly not impossible, is closer in magnitude of difficulty to performing a double bypass heart operation than to hammering a nail.[5]

The challenge to those deeply committed to school improvement, including researchers, teachers, administrators, and parents, is to acknowledge that both continuity and change are interwoven in the schooling process. To disentangle one from the other and attach positive or negative connotations is to misconstrue the very nature of schooling and classroom instruction. Those who have tried to convince teachers to adopt technological innovations over the last century have discovered the durablity of classroom pedagogy. Those fervent advocates who see the computer as the way to increase classroom productivity also will need to reckon with the enduring processes of constancy and change in public schools.

NOTES
BIBLIOGRAPHY
INDEX

Notes

INTRODUCTION

1. The Zachiarias quote comes from Charles Silberman, *Crisis in the Classroom* (New York: Random House, 1971), p. 171. See also Alan Gaynor, "The Study of Change in Educational Organizations: A Review of the Literature," in Luvern Cunningham and Donald Erickson (Eds.), *Educational Administration* (Berkeley, CA: McCutchan, 1977), pp. 234–259; Seymour Sarason, *The Culture of the School and the Problem of Change* (Boston: Allyn and Bacon, 1971); Robert Dreeben, "American Schooling: Patterns and Processes of Stability and Change," in Bernard Barber and Alex Inkeles, (Eds.), *Stability and Social Change* (Boston: Little, Brown, 1971); David Tyack et al., "Educational Reform: Retrospect and Prospect," *Teachers College Record* 81 (Spring 1980), pp. 253–269; W. Lynn McKinney and Ian Westbury, "Stability and Change: The Public Schools of Gary, Indiana, 1940–1970," in William Reid and Decker Walker (Eds.), *Case Studies in Curriculum Change* (London: Routledge and Kegan Paul, 1976); Larry Cuban, "Determinants of Curriculum Change and Stability, 1870–1970," in Jon Schafferzick and Gary Sykes (Eds.), *Value Conflicts and Curriculum Issues* (Berkeley, CA: McCutchan, 1979).
2. The Rickover quote comes from a prepared statement that he made before the Virginia State Board of Education on July 28, 1983, p. 1. For a typical article condemning faddism and inertia in the same piece, see Richard Hooper, "A Diagnosis of Failure," *AV Communication Review* (Fall 1969), p. 251.
3. Charles Hoban, "Instruction as a Systematic Approach to Instructional Technology," in Sidney Tickton (Ed.), *To Improve Learning*, (New York: Xerox Corp., 1971), vol. 2; Dave Berkman, "Instructional Television: The Medium Whose Future Has Passed?" *Educational Technology* (May 1976), pp. 39–44.

4. Goals for public schooling have been written about extensively: see Harvey Averch et al., *How Effective Is Schooling?* (Santa Monica, Ca: Rand Corp., 1972); Robert Dreeben, *On What Is Learned in School* (Menlo Park, CA: Addison-Wesley, 1968); Stanley Elam (Ed.), *A Decade of Gallup Polls of Attitudes Toward Education, 1969–1978* (Bloomington, IN: Phi Delta Kappa, 1978).

5. Lee Shulman, "Autonomy and Obligation: The Remote Control of Teaching," in Lee Shulman and Gary Sykes (Eds.), *Handbook on Teaching and Policy* (New York: Longman, 1983); Robert Dreeben, "The School as a Workplace," in W. Traver (Ed.), *The Second Handbook of Teaching* (New York: Rand McNally, 1973); Larry Cuban, *How Teachers Taught: Constancy and Change in American Classrooms, 1890–1980* (New York: Longman, 1984).

6. The Whitehead quote is cited in George Gordon, *Educational Television* (New York: Center for Applied Research on Education, 1965), p. 1.

7. Ray Callahan, *Education and the Cult of Efficiency* (Chicago: University of Chicago Press, 1962), chaps. 4–7.

8. Philip Jackson, *The Teacher and the Machine* (Pittsburgh: University of Pittsburgh Press, 1966), pp. 31–36; Martin Trow, "The New Media in the Evolution of American Education," in Peter Rossi and Bruce Biddle (Eds.), *The New Media and Education* (Chicago: Aldine, 1966), p. 325; Henry McCusker and Philip Sorensen, "The Economics of Education," in Rossi and Biddle, p. 188; Stephen Knezevich (Ed.), *Instructional Technology and the School Administration* (Washington, D.C.: American Association of School Administrators, 1970), pp. 21–23; Sidney Tickton (Ed.), *To Improve Learning* (New York: Xerox Corp., 1971), vol. 1, p. 10.

9. For other conventional definitions, see Knezevich, p. 13, and Tickton, vol. 1, p. 21. For a broader definition, see Everett M. Rogers, *Diffusion of Innovations* (New York: Free Press, 1983), p. 12.

10. Poem is from Virginia Church, *Teachers Are People, Being the Lyrics of Agatha Brown, Sometime Teacher in the Hilldale High School* (Hollywood, CA: David Fischer Corp., 1925), quoted in David Tyack, "Educational Moonshot," *Kappan* (February 1977), p. 457. For sources that comment on the cycles that have occurred with other technological innovations, see Hayden Smith, "What's Wrong with ITV," *Education* (February 1969), pp. 257–259; Ralph Tyler, "Utilization of Technological Media, Devices, and Systems in the Schools," *Educational Technology* (January 1980), pp. 11–15. For assessment of film use and other technologies used in classrooms, see

Anthony Oettinger and Sema Marks, "Educational Technology: New Myths and Old Realities," *Harvard Educational Review* 38 (Fall 1968), pp. 697–717; Edgar Dale, "Impact of New Media in the Secondary School Curriculum," in George Z. F. Bereday and Joseph A. Lauwerys (Eds.), *The Year Book of Education, 1958* (London: University of London Institute of Education, 1958), pp. 304–317.

To give a more concrete picture of popular and academic interest in instructional television, Lesley Taylor, a Stanford University graduate student, counted articles in the *Education Index* and *Readers' Guide to Periodical Literature*. The results are as follows:

	Number of Articles	
Years	Ed. Index	Readers' Guide
1950–1955	491	175
1955–1960	624	240
1960–1965	795	142
1965–1970	809	128
1970–1975	667	82
1975–1980	501	57

Milton Chen, another Stanford graduate student, prepared a report of the data base that Educational Resources Information Center (ERIC) uses. ERIC publishes *Resources in Education* (RIE) and *Current Index to Resources in Education* (CIRE). He found that studies of instructional television hit a high mark of popularity in 1971 with 371 studies, falling to 111 in 1981, and only 50 in 1982.

11. To answer these questions, a brief description of my research methods would be appropriate. I completed a review of the academic research and popular literature on the adoption, use, and influence of classroom media since 1920. This review included controlled experiments, impressionistic accounts, surveys, interviews, project reports, ethnographies, and combinations of these approaches. In examining this diverse body of formal and informal research, I avoided a meta-analysis of comparable studies and concentrated on making sense of the conclusions.

Magazine articles, impressionistic recollections, and promotional literature were read but were excluded from this analysis except for those accounts written by teachers and principals describing their use of machines. In sorting out the various types of research, surveys clearly dominated the field. Almost a cliché in such summaries of studies, I found the usual range in quality of the reported research. For instructional television research, I decided to include those surveys that used established canons for selecting the sample, reported acceptable ranges for response rates, and explicitly acknowledged issues of reliability and validity. Applying these minimum criteria severely reduced the number of studies for television and virtually eliminated studies reporting teacher use of radio and motion pictures. For the latter media, I relaxed the criteria in order to get some data on teacher use. Wherever possible, for these studies I state who responded and detail the response rate, if provided.

Most surveys were simply homemade questionnaires sent to administrators and occasionally to teachers. Responses from whomever took the time to answer were tallied and reported as findings. Moreover, in the gush of enthusiasm for the innovation, broad liberties often were taken with these fragmentary data: for example, they were used to justify expansion of services or as a rationale for seeking additional funds. See, for example, Dave Berkman's article (cited in note 3) of two instances of how statistics are misused to inflate overall reports of teacher usage (pp. 43–44). Also, Ronald Gross and Judith Murphy ("The Unfilled Promise of ITV," *Saturday Review*, November 19, 1966, pp. 88–89) cite another instance of overestimation. In short, the quality of research is seriously flawed.

While I applied these minimum criteria, let me make clear that this review is not a comprehensive, critical analysis of media research. From the studies I did analyze, I prepared estimates of the level of media influence upon classroom practice and noted the patterns of use that had been reported. Then I pulled from a number of qualitative studies (e.g., first-hand accounts and ethnographies) assessments of influence on teaching practice. I compared the results from these two different sets of findings in order to develop a more refined estimate of teacher use.

For instructional television, I went one step further. I identified a number of schools in the San Jose and San Francisco areas that had reputations for sustained video use, ample equipment, and administrators who encouraged classroom television. In short, I sought exemplars of school and teacher use in order to see if the research findings drawn from the literature resembled what existed in schools noted for their affection toward the medium. I wanted to see how many, if any, gaps existed between what research reported and what I saw in schools where influence was acknowledged, nourished, and praised.

CHAPTER 1

Epigraph source: Harry A. Wise, *Motion Pictures as an Aid in Teaching American History* (New Haven, CT: Yale University Press, 1939), p. 1.

1. Barbara Finkelstein, *Governing the Young: Teacher Behavior in American Primary Schools, 1820–1880* (Unpublished Ed.D. dissertation, Teachers College, Columbia University, 1970), p. 22. See also Joseph Rice, *The Public School System of the United States* (New York: Arno Press, 1969).
2. Such photos can be seen in the Frances Benjamin Johnson collection of photographs lodged in the Library of Congress. I have reproduced those and similar ones in Cuban, *How Teachers Taught.*
3. Portland School District, *Report of the Survey of the Public School System of School District No. 1, Multnomah County, Oregon* (November 1, 1913), p. 119.
4. Romiett Stevens, *The Question as a Measure of Efficiency in Instruction* (New York: Bureau of Publications, Teachers College, Columbia University, 1912), pp. 11, 15–17.
5. See Harold Rugg, *The Child-Centered School* (Yonkers-on-the-Hudson, NY: World Book Co., 1928); Agnes DeLima, *Our Enemy the Child* (New York: New Republic, 1925); Cuban, *How Teachers Taught,* chap. 2.
6. See Callahan; David Tyack, *The One Best System* (Cambridge, MA: Harvard University Press, 1974), especially pp. 126–147 and 182–198.
7. *Time,* October 31, 1938, p. 31.
8. *Dramatic Mirror,* July 9, 1913, cited in Paul Saettler, *A History of Instructional Technology* (New York: McGraw-Hill, 1968), p. 98.
9. James Kinder and F. Dean McClusky (Eds.), *The Audio-Visual Reader* (Dubuque, IA: Wm. C. Brown, 1954), p. 103; W. C. Meierhenry, "Some Historical and Current Developments in Motion Pictures," in *Educational Media Yearbook, 1982* (Littleton, CO: Libraries Unlimited, 1982), p. 75.
10. Saettler, pp. 98, 118; Kinder and McClusky, p. 33.

11. See Meierhenry article: Saettler, pp. 98–115: Kinder and Mc-Clusky, pp. 103–105.

12. A summary of the research until 1934 can be found in *Aids to Teaching in the Elementary School*, 13th Yearbook of the National Elementary School Principals Association (Washington, D.C.: National Education Association, 1934), chap. 10. See also Wise, pp. 4–25.

13. *Aids to Teaching in the Elementary Schools*, p. 151.

14. National Education Association, "Audio-Visual Education in City School Systems," *Research Bulletin* 24 (December 1946), pp. 134, 146–148.

15. National Education Association, "Audio-Visual Education in Urban School Districts, 1953–1954," *Research Bulletin* 33 (October 1955), pp. 93, 114.

16. Dale, pp. 304–305.

17. Mark May and Arthur Lumsdaine, *Learning from Films* (New Haven, CT: Yale University Press, 1958), p. 206.

18. NEA, *Research Bulletin* (1955), p. 105: Kinder and McClusky, p. 293.

19. NEA, *Research Bulletin* (1946), pp. 165–168: Kinder and McClusky, p. 115: May and Lumsdaine, pp. 300–304.

20 Benjamin Darrow, *Radio: The Assistant Teacher* (Columbus, OH: R. G. Adams, 1932), p. 79.

21. William Levenson, *Teaching Through Radio* (New York: Farrar and Rinehart, 1945), p. 457.

22. See Carroll Atkinson, *Development of Radio Education Policies in American School Systems* (Edinboro, PA: Edinboro Educational Press, 1939), pp. 3–8: Levenson, pp. 24–30: Saettler, pp. 201–226.

23. Atkinson, p. 41: Levenson, pp. 31–32: Norman Woelfel and Keith Tyler, *Radio and the School* (Yonkers-on-the-Hudson, NY: World Book Co., 1945), p. 89.

24. Atkinson, pp. 129–132.

25. Woelfel and Tyler, p. 1.

26. Lelia Ormsby, *Audio Education in the Public Schools of California* (Unpublished dissertaton, Stanford University, 1948), pp. 87–96.

27. Woelfel and Tyler, p. 57.

28. Atkinson, pp. 12–13.

29. Woelfel and Tyler, pp. 80–81.

30. Ibid., pp. 60–61.

31. Carroll Atkinson, *Education by Radio in American Schools*

(Nashville, TN: George Peabody College for Teachers, 1938),
pp. 38–39.

32. Woelfel and Tyler, pp. 2–3.

33. Wisconsin Research Project in School Broadcasting, *Radio in the Classroom* (Madison, WI: The University of Wisconsin Press, 1942), pp. 174–175.

34. Levenson, pp. 203–206.

35. Ibid., p. 181.

36. Woelfel and Tyler, p. 2.

37. Ibid., p. 3.

38. Ibid., pp. 4–5.

39. Kinder and McClusky, p. 157.

40. Darrow, p. 266.

CHAPTER 2

Research assistant Lesley Taylor helped draft the section of this chapter entitled "Impact of Instructional Television on the Classroom Teacher."

1. For more information on the introduction of classroom television, see Richard Hull, "A Note on the History Behind ETV," in Wilbur Schramm (Ed.), *Educational Television: The Next Ten Years*, pp. 334–345; Gordon, pp. 4–14; Robert Carlson, "Educator vs. Broadcaster in Development of ETV," *Educational Technology*, July 1971, pp. 13–16; Carroll Newsom (Ed.), *A Television Policy for Education* (Washington, D.C.: American Council on Education, 1952), pp. 118–119.

2. *Teaching by Television* (New York: Ford Foundation, 1961), pref., p. 5; Saettler, p. 237.

3. "Educational Broadcasting Facility Program: Grants for Education and Radio," *American Education* 7 (November 1971), p. 24; American Council on Education, "Special Report on Federal Programs," cited in *Educational Record* 44 (October 1963), p. 385.

4. Wilbur Schramm, Lyle M. Nelson, and Mere T. Betham, *Bold Experiment* (Stanford, CA: Stanford University Press, 1981).

5. I have borrowed the four patterns used by Keith Tyler and telescoped them into three. For a discussion of Tyler's patterns, see Henry Cassirer, *Television Teaching Today* (Paris: UNESCO, 1960), p. 53–54.

6. Schramm, Nelson, and Betham, p. 64.

7. Ibid., p. 48.
8. Ibid., pp. 54–55.
9. Ibid., pp. 81–89.
10. Ibid., p. 185.
11. *Teaching by Television*, p. 45.
12. David Lyle, *Washington County Closed Circuit Television Report* (Hagerstown, Maryland: Washington County, Maryland Board of Education, n.d.), p. 16, Table A. Also, telephone interview with Mr. Bill Kercheval, Director of Department of Instructional Television, Washington County, March 30, 1983.
13. Lyle, pp. 15–16.
14. Cassirer, p. 37; "Testimony of William Brish, Washington County (Md.) Superintendent," in Schramm, p. 82.
15. Lyle, pp. 44–72.
16. Telephone interview with Bill Kercheval, March 30, 1983.
17. See previously cited articles by Ralph Tyler ("Utilization of Technological Media, Devices, and Systems in the Schools") and David Tyack et al. ("Educational Reform: Retrospect and Prospect"). See also Neal Gross, Joseph B. Giacquinta, and Marilyn Bernstein, *Implementing Organizational Innovations* (New York: Basic Books, 1971); Harry Wolcott, *Teachers and Technocrats* (Eugene, OR: Center for Educational Policy and Management, University of Oregon, 1977).
18. See Harry Wolcott, "Is There Life After Technology? Some Lessons on Change," *Educational Technology* (May 1981), pp. 24–28.
19. Wilbur Schramm, "What We Know About Instructional Television," in Schramm, pp. 52–76. See also Godwin Chu and Wilbur Schramm, "Learning from Television: What the Research Says," in Tickton, vol. 1, pp. 179–182.
20. Harry Kincaid et al., *Technology in Public Elementary and Secondary Education: A Policy Analysis Perspective* (Menlo Park, CA: Stanford Research Institute, 1974), p. 6.
21. R. W. Faunce, *Use of, and Reaction To, Educational Television Lessons (KTCA, Channel 2) by Minneapolis Elementary School Teachers, 1970–71* (Minneapolis: Minneapolis Special School District 1, June 1971), ERIC Document Reproduction Service No. ED 069 142; John Willis, *The Use of Instructional Television in West Virginia Elementary Schools, 1977–1978* (Charleston: West Virginia State Department of Education, Bureau of Planning, Research, and Evaluation, October 1978), ERIC Document Reproduction Service No. ED 168 554; Kerry

Johnson and Paul Keller, *Television in the Public Schools. Final Report of the Maryland ITV Utilization Study* (College Park: Maryland University, School of Library and Information Services, December 1981), ERIC Document Reproduction Service No. ED 213 394.

22. Peter Dirr and Ronald Pedone, "A National Report on the Use of Instructional Television," *AV Instruction* (January 1978). See also Johnson and Keller, p. 19.

23. Dirr and Pedone, pp. 9, 13.

24. Ibid., pp. 9–10.

25. James Sanders and Subhash Sonnad, *Research in the Introduction, Use, and Impact of the "Thinkabout" Instructional Television Series,* Technical Report, vol. 1 (Bloomington, IN: Agency for Instructional Television, 1982), p. 114.

26. Harry Wolcott, *A View of Viewers: Observations on the Response to and Classroom Use of "Thinkabout,"* Technical Report, vol. 4 (Bloomington, IN: Agency for Instructional Television, 1982), pp. 1–3, 44; Sanders and Sonnad, p. 9.

27. Marilyn Cohn, *Teacher Use and Student Response in Three Classrooms,* Technical Report, vol. 2 (Bloomington, IN: Agency for Instructional Television, 1982); Sylvia Hart-Landsberg, *Toward a Clear Picture of "Thinkabout": An Account of Classroom Use,* Technical Report, vol. 3 (Bloomington, IN: Agency for Instructional Television, 1982); Wolcott, *A View of Viewers.*

28. Wolcott, *A View of Viewers,* pp. 13, 99.

29. Gross and Murphy, p. 88.

CHAPTER 3

Epigraph source: Javad Maftoon, "ITV: Are Teachers Using It?" *T. H. E. Journal* (February 1982), p. 45.

1. The comparison to a man kissing his wife comes from A. J. Liebling, *The Press* (New York: Ballantine, 1975), p. 29.

2. Gross and Murphy, p. 103.

3. Tickton, vol. 1, p. 79.

4. Willis.

5. Johnson and Keller, p. 24.

6. Morris Janowitz and David Street, "The Social Organization of Education," in Rossi and Biddle, p. 227. For teacher responses

to district, state, and federal innovations, see Milbrey McLaughlin, "Implementation as Mutual Adaptation in Classroom Organization," in Dale Mann (Ed.), *Making Change Happen* (New York: Teachers College Press, 1978). pp. 19–31; Michael Fullan, *The Meaning of Educational Change* (New York: Teachers College Press, 1982); Matthew Miles, "School Innovation from the Ground Up: Some Dilemmas," *New York University Education Quarterly* (Fall 1979), pp. 1–9.

7. Barker is quoted in Marianne Amarel, "Classrooms and Computers as Instructional Settings," *Theory into Practice* 22 (November 1983). pp. 260–266. The main thrust of this argument is drawn from Philip Jackson, *Life in Classrooms* (New York: Holt, Rinehart and Winston, 1968), chap. 1; Sarason, chaps. 1, 7, 10, 11; Louis Smith and William Geoffrey, *The Complexities of an Urban Classroom* (New York: Holt, Rinehart and Winston, 1968), chaps. 3–4; Robert Dreeben, "The School as a Workplace"; Hugh Mehan, *Learning Lessons* (Cambridge, MA: Harvard University Press, 1979), chap. 3; Cuban, *How Teachers Taught*, chap. 6.

8. Jackson, *Life in Classrooms*, p. 11.

9. Jackson, *The Teacher and the Machine*, p. 6.

10. Ibid.

11. Ibid., pp. 17–21. See also Dan Lortie, *Schoolteacher* (Chicago: University of Chicago Press, 1975).

12. The attitudes cited here were evident among both teachers and administrators in the interviews my assistant and I conducted in the two exemplary schools and another San Jose area school in which we piloted our questions with the teachers and the principal.

13. Hoban, p. 133.

14. Ibid.

15. See Willard Waller, *The Sociology of Teaching* (New York: Wiley, 1965), chaps. 22–23; Lortie, chaps. 2–3; Estelle Fuchs, *Teacher Talk* (New York: Anchor Books, 1969).

16. Cuban, *How Teachers Taught*.

17. The phrase "practicality ethic" comes from Walter Doyle and G. Ponder, "The Practicality Ethic in Teacher Decision Making," *Interchange* 8 (1977–1978), pp. 1–12. Everett Rogers uses the concept of compatibility to mean roughly the same thing; see *Diffusion of Innovations*, pp. 223–226.

18. For teachers and administrators who advocated frequent use of instructional and commercial television in classrooms, see

Rosemary Lee Potter, *New Season: The Positive Use of Commercial Television with Children* (Columbus, OH: Charles Merrill, 1976); Robert Hilliard and Hyman Field, *Television and the Teacher: A Handbook for Classroom Use* (New York: Hastings House, 1976). For a description of a "willing user," see the description of Mr. Cartwright, a sixth-grade teacher, in Cohn, pp. 93–140.

19. Harry Wolcott's discussion of the use of "Thinkabout" called to my attention this point concerning teacher energy rhythm. Our interviews at Pine and Spruce schools repeatedly turned up references by teachers to the ebb and flow of the school day. Such a common issue also may explain the long-standing use of Fridays as a test and film day.

20. The articles by Oettinger and Marks and Ralph Tyler, already cited, and the work of Robert Dreeben and Philip Jackson emphasize these points. Milbrey McLaughlin's work on responses to innovation supports this perspective as well.

CHAPTER 4

Epigraph sources: Seymour Papert, "Trying to Predict the Future," *Popular Computing*, October 1984, p. 38; Dale Peterson, "Nine Issues," *Popular Computing*, October 1984, p. 11. I selected these two epigraph quotes to demonstrate anew the ambitious claims of classroom computer advocates, as well as to suggest the skeptical note in their claims. Throughout this chapter, I will refer to "boosters," "enthusiasts," and "advocates" of classroom computers. While there is clearly a large number of supporters for instructional use of computers located in universities, school districts, corporate offices, and foundations, I do not suggest a monolithic view on how and why the machines are to be used. One wing of the advocates trace their origins back to enthusiasm for most forms of machine technology (e.g., television, radio, films, language laboratories, CAI, etc.) as being far more efficient and effective in classrooms than teachers talking. The engineering orientation is most strong among the "ed techies." Another group of advocates is far more ambitious about the power of the computer and wishes to see the school, as it is currently organized, transformed into a learning environment anchored in computer technology. Yet another group sees the computerization of schools as necessary to their being relevant to society, but they also recognize that, while computer entry into schools may be slow and the uses of the machines may be unimaginative initially, this evolutionary pace is still worthwhile. Thus, while I will use such labels as "enthusiasts," readers should know that diverse views exist amidst the many who desire more instructional uses for computers.

1. "Here Come the Microkids," *Time*, May 3, 1982, pp. 50–56.
2. Editorial, *Popular Computing*, August 1983, p. 83.
3. Joe Nathan, "Viewpoint," *InfoWorld*, July 25, 1983, p. 35.
4. Burt Schorr, "Many Schools Buying Computers Find Problems with Using Them," *Wall Street Journal*, April 7, 1983, p. 1: Edward Fiske, "Computer Education: Update '83," *Popular Computing*, August 1983, pp. 86–96, 142–147.
5. Edward Feigenbaum and Pamela McCorduck, *The Fifth Generation* (Boston: Addison-Wesley, 1983), p. 233.
6. See Rogers, chaps. 6, 7, 9, and 11. I chose these questions and not others because of the direction of my own research.
7. Milton Chen and William Paisley, "Children and the New Computer Technologies: Research Implications of the Second Electronic Revolution," in *Mass Communication Review Yearbook*, vol. 7 (Beverly Hills, CA: Sage, in press).
8. Decker Walker, "Promise, Potential, and Pragmatism: Computers in High School," *IFG Policy Notes* (Summer 1984), p. 3. See also Decker Walker, "Reflections on the Educational Potential and Limitations of Microcomputers," *Kappan* 64 (October 1983), pp. 103–107.
9. Fiske, p. 89.
10. In May and June of 1983, I visited seven high schools in California, Nevada, and Arizona that had been nominated as exemplary by the U.S. Department of Education, in a national effort to recognize effective secondary schools. My impressions are drawn from those schools' programs in beginning and sustaining computers in classrooms. Supplementing these impressions were my many visits to San Francisco and San Jose area schools.
11. See Richard Shavelson et al., *"Successful" Teachers' Patterns of Microcomputer-Based Mathematics and Science Instruction: A Rand Note* (Santa Monica, CA: Rand Corp., 1984); Gail Meister, *Successful Integration of Microcomputers in an Elementary School*, Project Report No. 84-A13 (Stanford, CA: Institute for Research on Educational Finance and Governance, 1984).

12. For a study that reveals some of the different approaches districts have taken to introducing and sustaining machine use in classrooms, see Karen Sheingold et al., "Microcomputer Use in Schools: Developing a Research Agenda," *Harvard Educational Review* 53 (November 1983), pp. 412–432.

13. See Walker, "Promise, Potential, and Pragmatism," pp. 3–4, and Sheingold article cited above.

14. National Center of Educational Statistics, *Instructional Use of Computers in Public Schools* (Washington, D.C.: U.S. Department of Education, 1982), pp. 1–2.

15. *Education Week*, April 18, 1984, pp. 1, 14.

16. *Education Week*, March 27, 1985, p. 6.

17. *Education Week*, July 27, 1983, p. 7.

18. Shavelson et al., pp. 33–49.

19. Sheingold, pp. 426–427; Robert Hess and Irene Miura, "Access," *IFG Policy Notes* (Summer 1984), pp. 4–5.

20. Charles Euchner, "Teachers' Interest in Computers Is High, but Usage Is Low," *Education Week*, January 12, 1983, p. 5.

21. "Thomas Dwyer," in Robert Taylor (Ed.), *The Computer in the School: Tutor, Tool, Tutee* (New York: Teachers College Press, 1980), pp. 96, 114.

22. Seymour Papert, *Mindstorms: Children, Computers, and Powerful Ideas* (New York: Basic Books, 1980), pp. 177–187. Pat Suppes also predicted that teaching would change as computers penetrated schools in "The Uses of Computers in Education," *Scientific American* 215 (September 1966), pp. 218–219.

23. Taylor, pp. 1–10. Also see experience of Scarsdale, New York, as reported in Charles Euchner, "A District Learns to 'Debug' Its Curriculum," *Education Week*, December 15, 1982, p. 6.

24. Harriet Cuffaro, "Microcomputers in Education: Why Is Earlier Better?" *Teachers College Record* 85 (Summer 1984), p. 560.

25. Henry Levin, Gene V. Glass, and Gail R. Meister, *Cost Effectiveness of Four Educational Interventions*, Project Report No. 84–A11 (Stanford, CA: Institute for Research on Educational Finance and Governance, 1984).

26. Ibid., pp. 3–4.

27. Ibid., p. 30.

28. Ibid., pp. 30–31.

29. Callahan, chaps. 4–5. See also Tyack, *The One Best System*, pp. 129–147, 182–216.

30. Arthur Wise, *Legislated Learning* (Berkeley, CA: University of California Press, 1979), chaps. 2–4; Larry Cuban, "Trans-

forming the Frog into a Prince: Effective Schools Research, Policy, and Practice at the District Level," *Harvard Educational Review* 54 (May 1984), pp. 129–151.

31. Jackson, *Life in Classrooms,* chaps. 4–5; Elliot Eisner, "On the Uses of Educational Connoisseurship and Criticism for Evaluating Classroom Life," *Teachers College Record* 78 (Fall 1977), pp. 345–358.

32. Douglas Sloan, "On Raising Critical Questions about the Computer in Education," *Teachers College Record* 85 (Summer 1984), pp. 539–545.

33. Jackson, *Life in Classrooms,* chap. 4; Lortie, pp. 101–108.

34. This issue of machine-student bonds is explored in Sherry Turkle, *The Second Self: Computers and the Human Spirit* (New York: Simon and Schuster, 1984), chaps. 1 and 3.

35. Jackson, *Life in Classrooms,* p. 175.

36. For descriptions of theories, see N. L. Gage and David Berliner, *Educational Psychology* (Boston: Houghton Mifflin, 1984), chaps. 11–15.

37. These quesions are raised in Hubert Dreyfus and Stuart Dreyfus, "Putting Computers in Their Proper Place: Analysis Versus Intuition in the Classroom," *Teachers College Record* 85 (Summer 1984), pp. 587–601.

38. Papert, *Mindstorms,* pp. 173–176; Cuffaro, p. 560; John Davy, "Mindstorms in the Lamplight," *Teachers College Record* 85 (Summer 1984), pp. 549–558.

39. Joseph Weizenbaum, in an interview with Franz-Olivier Giesbert of *Le Nouvel Observateur,* December 2, 1983, cited in *Harper's,* March 1984, p. 22.

40. Walker, "Promise, Potential, and Pragmatism," p. 3; Mary Alice White, "Synthesis of Research on Electronic Learning," *Educational Leadership* (May 1983), pp. 13–15; Stanley Pogrow, "Linking Technology Use to School Improvement," in Allan Odden and L. Dean Webb (Eds.), *School Finance and School Improvement* (Cambridge, MA: Ballinger, 1983), pp. 133–135.

41. Cited in Cuffaro, p. 567.

42. Cuffaro, p. 561.

43. Ibid.

44. Davy, p. 550.

45. Ibid., p. 554.

46. Ibid.

47. Joseph Weizenbaum, *Computer Power and Human Reason* (San Francisco: W. H. Freeman, 1976), pp. 248–256.

48. Art Buchwald, cited in *Calendar of Quotes, 1984* (New York: Workman, 1983).
49. Turkle, p. 59.
50. Ibid., p. 135.
51. Ibid., pp. 129–134.
52. While I am prepared to support the suggested reforms listed here, I use them now only to illustrate the constricted views that advocates of technology hold on school improvement. The notion that fundamental school changes would require enormous outlays in tax revenues is either beyond the pale for reformers imbued with visions of technological cures or secretly acknowledged but not explicitly voiced.
53. Richard Lyons, "How Mental Patients' Release Began," *New York Times*, October 30, 1984, sec. 3, p. 1.
54. Ibid.
55. Ibid.

EPILOGUE

1. For a concise summary of school reform, see Tyack et al., pp. 253–269.
2. The concept of stable processes of change as I use it comes from James G. March, "Footnotes to Organizational Change," *Administrative Science Quarterly* 26 (December 1981), 563–577.
3. Edward Spicer (Ed.), *Human Problems in Technological Change* (New York: Russell Sage Foundation, 1952), p. 294.
4. Wolcott, "Is There Life After Technology?" p. 25.
5. Michael Fullan, in *The Meaning of Educational Change*, deals with many issues linked to altering teacher behavior; see chap. 7.

Bibliography

Atkinson, Carroll. *Development of Radio Education Policies in American School Systems.* Edinboro, PA: Edinboro Educational Press, 1939.

———. *Education by Radio in American Schools.* Nashville, TN: George Peabody College for Teachers, 1938.

Callahan, Raymond. *Education and the Cult of Efficiency.* Chicago: University of Chicago Press, 1962.

Cassirer, Henry. *Television Teaching Today.* Paris: UNESCO, 1960.

Cuban, Larry. *How Teachers Taught: Constancy and Change in American Classrooms, 1890–1980.* New York: Longman, 1984.

Cuffaro, Harriet. "Microcomputers in Education: Why Is Earlier Better?" *Teachers College Record* 85 (Summer 1984), pp. 559–568.

Darrow, Benjamin. *Radio: The Assistant Teacher.* Columbus, OH: R. G. Adams, 1932.

Davy, John. "Mindstorms in the Lamplight." *Teachers College Record* 85 (Summer 1984), pp. 549–558.

Dirr, Peter, and Ronald Pedone. "A National Report on the Use of Instructional Television." *AV Instruction* (January 1978), pp. 11–13.

Doyle, Walter, and G. Ponder. "The Practicality Ethic in Teacher Decision Making." *Interchange* 8 (1977–1978), pp. 1–12.

Dreyfus, Hubert, and Stuart Dreyfus. "Putting Computers in Their Proper Place: Analysis Versus Intuition in the Classroom." *Teachers College Record* 85 (Summer 1984), pp. 578–601.

Euchner, Charles. "Teachers' Interest in Computers Is High, but Usage Is Low." *Education Week*, January 12, 1983, p. 5.

Faunce, R. W. *Use of, and Reaction to, Educational Television Lessons (KTCA, Channel 2) by Minneapolis Elementary School Teachers, 1970–71.* Minneapolis: Minneapolis Special School

District 1, June 1971. (ERIC Document Reproduction Service No. ED 069 142)

Fullan, Michael. *The Meaning of Educational Change*. New York: Teachers College Press, 1982.

Gordon, George. *Educational Television*. New York: Center for Applied Research, 1965.

Gross, Neal, Joseph B. Giacquinta, and Marilyn Bernstein. *Implementing Organizational Innovations*. New York: Basic Books, 1971.

Jackson, Philip. *Life in Classrooms*. New York: Holt, Rinehart and Winston, 1968.

Johnson, Kerry, and Paul Keller. *Television in the Public Schools, Final Report of the Maryland ITV Utilization Study*. College Park: Maryland University, School of Library and Information Services, December 1981. (ERIC Document Reproduction Service No. ED 213-394)

Kinder, James, and F. Dean McClusky (Eds.). *The Audio-Visual Reader*. Dubuque, IA: William C. Brown, 1954.

Levenson, William. *Teaching Through Radio*. New York: Farrar and Rinehart, 1945.

Levin, Henry, Gene V. Glass, and Gail R. Meister. *Cost Effectiveness of Four Educational Interventions*. Project Report No. 84-A11. Stanford, CA: Institute for Research on Educational Finance and Governance, 1984.

March, James G. "Footnotes to Organizational Change." *Administrative Science Quarterly* 26 (December 1981), pp. 563–577.

May, Mark, and Arthur Lumsdaine. *Learning from Films*. New Haven, CT: Yale University Press, 1958.

McLaughlin, Milbrey. "Implementation as Mutual Adaptation in Classroom Organization." In *Making Change Happen*, edited by Dale Mann. New York: Teachers College Press, 1978.

Meierhenry, W. C. "Some Historical and Current Developments in Motion Pictures." In *Educational Media Yearbook*, 1982. Littleton, CO: Libraries Unlimited, 1982.

Meister, Gail. *Successful Integration of Microcomputers in an Elementary School*. Project Report No. 84-A13. Stanford, CA: Institute for Research on Educational Finance and Governance, 1984.

National Education Association. "Audio-Visual Education in City School Systems." *Research Bulletin* 24 (December 1946), pp. 131–170.

National Education Association. "Audio-Visual Education in Urban School Districts, 1953–1954." *Research Bulletin* 33 (October 1955), pp. 91–123.

Pogrow, Stanley. "Linking Technology Use to School Improvement." In *School Finance and School Improvement*, edited by Allan Odden and L. Dean Webb. Cambridge, MA: Ballinger, 1983.

Saettler, Paul. *A History of Instructional Technology.* New York: McGraw-Hill, 1968.

Sanders, James, and Subhash Sonnad. *Research in the Introduction, Use, and Impact of the "Thinkabout" Instructional Television Series.* Technical Report, Volume 1. Bloomington, IN: Agency for Instructional Television, 1982.

Schramm, Wilbur, Lyle M. Nelson, Mere T. Betham. *Bold Experiment.* Stanford, CA: Stanford University Press, 1981.

Shavelson, Richard, John D. Winkler, Cathleen Stasz, Werner Feibel, Abby E. Robyn, and Steven Shaha. *"Successful" Teachers' Patterns of Microcomputer-Based Mathematics and Science Instruction: A Rand Note.* Santa Monica, CA: The Rand Corporation, 1984.

Sheingold, Karen, Janet H. Kane, and Mari E. Endreweit. "Microcomputer Use in Schools: Developing a Research Agenda." *Harvard Educational Review* 53 (November 1983), pp. 412–432.

Sloan, Douglas. "On Raising Critical Questions About the Computer in Education." *Teachers College Record* 85 (Summer 1984), pp. 539–547.

Spicer, Edward (Ed.). *Human Problems in Technological Change.* New York: Russell Sage Foundation, 1952.

Teaching by Television. New York: The Ford Foundation, 1961.

Tyack, David. *The One Best System.* Cambridge, MA: Harvard University Press, 1974.

Walker, Decker. "Promise, Potential, and Pragmatism: Computers in High School." *IFG Policy Notes* (Summer 1984).

Waller, Willard. *The Sociology of Teaching.* New York: Wiley, 1965.

Weizenbaum, Joseph. *Computer Power and Human Reason.* San Francisco: W. H. Freeman, 1976.

White, Mary Alice. "Synthesis of Research on Electronic Learning." *Educational Leadership* (May 1983), pp. 13–15.

Willis, John. *The Use of Instructional Television in West Virginia Elementary Schools, 1977–1978.* Charleston: West Virginia State Department of Education, Bureau of Planning, Research, and Evaluation, October 1978. (ERIC Document Reproduction Service No. ED 168 554)

Wisconsin Research Project in School Broadcasting. *Radio in the Classroom*. Madison, WI: The University of Wisconsin Press, 1942.

Wise, Arthur. *Legislated Learning*. Berkeley, CA: University of California Press, 1979.

Wise, Harry A. *Motion Pictures as an Aid in Teaching American History*. New Haven, CT: Yale University Press, 1939.

Woelfel, Norman, and Keith Tyler. *Radio and the School*. Yonkers-on-the-Hudson, NY: World Book Co., 1945.

Wolcott, Harry. "Is There Life After Technology? Some Lessons on Change." *Educational Technology* (May 1981), pp. 24–28.

———. *Teachers and Technocrats*. Eugene, OR: Center for Educational Policy and Management, University of Oregon, 1977.

———. *A View of Viewers: Observations on the Response to and Classroom Use of "Thinkabout."* Technical Report, Volume 4. Bloomington, IN: Agency for Instructional Television, 1982.

Index